Make *Training* EVALUATION Work

- Show Value and Communicate Results

- Select the Right Model and Find Resources

- Get Management Buy-In and Overcome Resistance

JACK J. PHILLIPS

PATRICIA PULLIAM PHILLIPS

TONI KRUCKY HODGES

ASTD Press

ASTD Press is an internationally renowned source of insightful and practical information on workplace learning and per-formance topics, including training basics, evaluation and return-on-investment (ROI), instructional systems development (ISD), e-learning, leadership, and career development.

Ordering information: Books published by ASTD Press can be purchased by visiting our Website at store.astd.org or by call-ing 800.628.2783 or 703.683.8100.

Library of Congress Control Number: 2004109345

ISBN: 1-56286-349-5

Acquisitions and Development Editor: Mark Morrow
Copyeditor: Karen Eddleman
Interior Design and Production: Kathleen Schaner
Cover Design: David Cooper
Cover Illustration: Leon Zernitsky

Contents

Preface

Make Training Evaluation Work uses easy-to-understand principles, guidelines, and examples to guide both novice and expert evaluators toward successful integration of evaluation in their learning and development processes. The novice evaluator will learn how to start, staff, organize, implement, and gain support for evaluation. For the seasoned evaluator, this book provides helpful advice to build management support for evaluation, revitalize an existing evaluation effort, communicate evaluation data, and drive improvements based on evaluation data.

The book shows how to make evaluation an important part of the learning and development process, not simply an add-on process. Many books offer specific evaluation models or methodologies for evaluation. *Make Training Evaluation Work,* however, shows how to take an evaluation process and make it come to life in an organization with minimum time and resources. Moreover, it is written in an understandable and fundamental style and provides tips, techniques, and examples illustrating each key point.

Why This Book?

In the past 20 years, much has been written about evaluation in learning and development. Some practitioners are confused by having *too many* options and possibilities from which to choose. Each organization needs a process that works and adds value. Even the best evaluation model or framework is worthless unless it is implemented and supported in the organization.

This book focuses on two issues: how to make evaluation work and how to build the necessary support for the process. This book complements any of the major publications that present evaluation models and frameworks. It shows how to take the selected framework and make it function internally. For those organizations needing assistance getting started, this book is an indispensable guide to show how the evaluation function is organized, structured, and staffed to obtain maximum payoff. The tools and techniques offered are feasible to implement even in small organizations where there is no full-time evaluation staff. Large, more mature organizations can find hundreds of useful ideas to enhance the evaluation process and make it more relevant, focused, and effective.

The Authors' Perspective

We bring a combined experience of more than 50 years of evaluation. As practitioners, we have researched, explored, implemented, organized, and managed evaluation for many different organizations. All three of us now serve as consultants assisting organizations with this important issue—implementing a comprehensive measurement and evaluation system. Together we have experienced firsthand what works and what doesn't work when it comes to implementing evaluation. Collectively, our experience cuts across several different industries, our academic preparation includes crossover fields, and our consulting assignments involve practically every type of organization in some 30 different countries.

In addition, we offer many useful tools, templates, and ideas developed while working with our clients as they struggled with this important issue.

Acknowledgments From Jack Phillips

No book is a work of the authors alone and this one is no exception. Many individuals helped provide information directly and indirectly to make this a success. I would like to thank the many clients and colleagues who have invited us to work with them in the past decade. We learn as much from our clients as they learn from us, if not more. Their insight, wisdom, and ideas often appear in our next article, case study, workshop, or book. To the hundreds of wonderful clients, we owe them a huge debt of gratitude.

Much of our work was inspired by Donald Kirkpatrick who started it all in evaluation with his four-level framework. We have attempted to build on what he has created and has been accepted so well throughout the world. We are also inspired by the work of Jac Fitz-enz, who is a pioneer in measurement and evaluation in the human resources area. Jac's initial efforts in the early 1970s set the tone and pace for much of the HR evaluation and benchmarking available today. We consider both Don and Jac to be not only mentors, but also our friends and colleagues.

Thanks to Toni for her efforts to work with us on this publication. Toni has done a marvelous job of making the transition from full-time evaluation practitioner internally as manager of measurement at Bell Atlantic to a successful consultant in evaluation. Much appreciation goes to Jaime Beard who meticulously organized, prepared, and assisted in editing this manuscript. Jaime juggled many projects to keep this book on track. Katherine Sanner provided additional support and assistance throughout the development of the manuscript. Kat always accepts these projects with the most gracious attitude. Joyce Alff, our managing editor, made many helpful suggestions to make the manuscript a reality.

And, above all, many thanks goes to my partner, friend, and spouse, Patti Phillips, for her enduring support and encouragement as we continue to push the envelope in the measurement and evaluation field.

Acknowledgments From Patti Phillips

Evaluation is a critical part of the training process. Unfortunately, many organizations still struggle to integrate it into their daily routine. For those of you who have been tenacious in your efforts to make it work—thank you. You are the role models among your peers. By sharing your success with others, you give us all opportunity to learn. Among the models of evaluation implementation success are Debi Wallace of Wachovia Bank and Deb Wharff of the National Security Agency. Many thanks go to you for your willingness to share (what you can) with others in our field. Thank you also for your continuous support in all of our efforts.

Thanks also go to Jaime, Kat, and Joyce. You continue to hang in there with us, and we appreciate you! We also acknowledge our friends at ASTD who recognize the importance of measurement and evaluation in the industry and have made great efforts to stay on the cutting edge as the industry catches. As always, my thanks and love go to Jack who continues to be generous with his knowledge and wisdom. He is my inspiration.

Acknowledgments From Toni Hodges

I want to express my appreciation to many of my current clients, particularly those at Nextel Communications, TD Bank of Toronto, and BMW Manufacturing as well as my former colleagues at Bell Atlantic who have worked with me to implement unique evaluation solutions in their organizations. I also want to thank Evelyn Chalmers Krucky—my mother and my champion.

Jack J. Phillips
Patricia Pulliam Phillips
Toni Krucky Hodges

October 2004

Introduction

Status of Evaluation

Evaluation has made tremendous progress in the past 50 years. Advances in evaluation represent significant changes and evolution in the field, which build on Kirkpatrick's framework for training evaluation. Today, several major conferences are conducted each year on evaluation. Dozens of books have been written on evaluating learning and development alone. A professional organization (the ASTD ROI Network) exists to support learning evaluators. Workshops and other competency development opportunities are offered frequently around the world.

In its early development, evaluation was often thought of as an add-on activity after a project or program was implemented. Evaluation was needed to see if the program was effective. Sometimes, the requirement or request for evaluation came from a client or sponsor who was concerned about the results. Today, evaluation is positioned much differently. It is the first, as well as the last, part of the process.

No illustration depicts this change more clearly than figure I-1 does. This model, released in 2003 by the United States Government Accountability Office in its guidelines for assessing strategic training and development efforts in the federal government, shows that evaluation is not only an important part of the process but is integrated throughout the process. No longer considered an add-on activity, evaluation now connects to the front-end analysis, the design and development, and implementation.

This new model positions evaluation where it must be to enhance the value of learning and development. It replaces commonly used models in which evaluation is the add-on component.

The Flow of the Book

This book, which discusses the challenges facing evaluators, is divided into three parts. The first part, with three chapters, sets the stage for evaluation. Chapter 1 focuses on many of the problems inherent in current evaluation models. It provides a summary of evaluation failures so that they can be avoided in the future. Chapter 2 explores the myths and mysteries of evaluation. Many of these myths must be dispelled to make evaluation work in an organization. Chapter 3 shows the tremendous number of benefits that can be realized by investing more time, effort, and resources in evaluation.

Part two, consisting of three chapters, focuses on the fundamentals of starting, organizing, developing, and integrating evaluation into the organization using evaluation data. Chapter 4 focuses on getting started by addressing the important issues of selecting the right model; developing policy, practice, and philosophy; staffing the evaluation process; and other important issues. Chapter 5 focuses on two critical issues: developing the needed expertise and securing the appropriate resources for evaluation. The competencies needed for successful evaluation are always changing. This chapter explores ways by which these competencies can be acquired or developed. Chapter 6 explores the critical role of communicating results

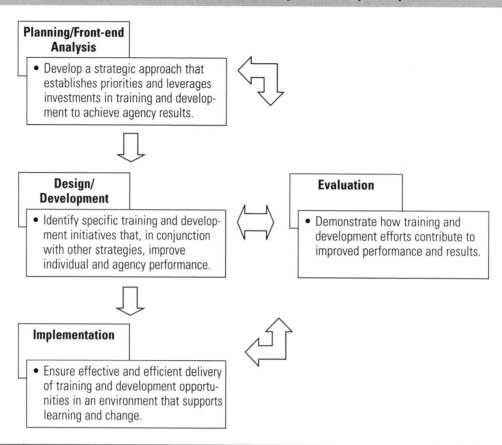

Figure I-1. Four components of the training and development process.

Planning/Front-end Analysis
- Develop a strategic approach that establishes priorities and leverages investments in training and development to achieve agency results.

Design/ Development
- Identify specific training and development initiatives that, in conjunction with other strategies, improve individual and agency performance.

Evaluation
- Demonstrate how training and development efforts contribute to improved performance and results.

Implementation
- Ensure effective and efficient delivery of training and development opportunities in an environment that supports learning and change.

Source: U.S. Government Accountability Office. (2003). *Human Capital: Guide for Strategic Training and Development Efforts.* GAO-03-893G. Washington, DC: GAO.

and evaluation information. Regardless of the evaluation process used, one of the important outcomes of evaluation is to make changes or improvements. To do this, a variety of target audiences need information to make decisions and take action. This chapter shows how to communicate data to target audiences and use that data to drive improvements and changes.

Part three, which encompasses three chapters, concentrates on making evaluation a successful, integral, and valued function in the organization. Chapter 7 focuses on the role of management and shows how to get management buy-in for evaluation. Management influence in learning and development and evaluation is critical. This chapter provides a variety of strategies, techniques, and tools to get managers involved and committed so that they reinforce, support, and enhance the evaluation process. Chapter 8 explores implementation

and shows how to overcome possible resistance to new or improved evaluation processes. It shows why resistance exists and discusses how the resistance can be minimized or removed entirely with dozens of tips, techniques, and strategies. Finally, chapter 9 focuses directly on ethics and standards, an often neglected part of the process. The ethical behavior of an evaluator is important as there are many ethical issues, challenges, and problems that can develop along the way. This chapter shows how to avoid ethical issues and develop standards for the evaluation process.

How to Use This Book

Because this book is developed in the sequence that evaluation is often implemented, it can be read sequentially. For those new to evaluation, it is recommended that each chapter be read in the order presented. For those familiar with evaluation, you may find it helpful to explore the chapters that meet your particular needs. Each chapter is developed as a stand-alone discussion for that particular topic. Scattered throughout the book are self-assessment tools, templates, and resources. Appendices add additional resources to top off a very useful and helpful guide.

About Terminology

Developing a book for learning and development always involves the difficult task of managing termi-

nology in a consistent manner. Table I-1 lists some important terms and defines how they are being used in this book.

Moving Forward

Now that you have a sense of this book's purpose and have a foundation in the vocabulary of evaluation, it's time to embark on part one, which focuses on attitudes or mindsets about evaluation and creates the proper mental framework to move forward with the rest of the book.

Table I-1. Key terms used in this book.

Term	Definition
Learning; Learning and Development	The activities for which evaluation is carried out. For any initiative, whether it is learning, training, development, or education, evaluation must occur. Other terms, such as *training* or *education* or *performance improvement* may be used interchangeably, but the evaluation methods are often the same.
Program	The specific entity being evaluated. It may be a one-week workshop, a six-month mentoring activity, or an online learning course. The term *program* is a more generic term than *course*, *activity*, *intervention*, or *process*.
Participant	An individual directly involved in the program. A participant is sometimes referred to as a delegate, attendee, or stakeholder.
Stakeholder	Any individual involved or interested in the program in some way. The list of stakeholders may include the participants, the facilitator, and the client, among others.
Client	The individual(s) who is funding, initiating, requesting, or supporting the particular learning and development program being evaluated. It is the key person or group, usually in the senior management team, who cares about the program's success and is in a position to stop the program or expand the program. The term *sponsor* is sometimes used.
Immediate Manager	The person in the organization one level above the person involved in the program. For some participants, the immediate manager would be the team leader, for others it is the middle manager, but, most important, the immediate manager is considered to be the person with supervisory authority over the participant in the program.
Chief Executive Officer (CEO)	The organization's top executive. The CEO could be a plant manager, division manager, the administrator for a large health care facility, or the agency head of a government organization. This person is the top administrator or executive in the operating entity where the learning and development program is being implemented.
Evaluator	The person conducting the evaluation. In most cases, this person is not a full-time evaluator but rather has part-time evaluation responsibilities. In larger organizations, this person has a full-time role and may even be the manager of evaluation.

Part One

Developing an Evaluation State of Mind

When you can measure what you are speaking about and express it in numbers, you know something about it; but when you cannot measure, when you cannot express it in numbers, your knowledge is of a meagre and unsatisfactory kind; it may be the beginning of knowledge, but you have scarcely in your thoughts advanced to the state of science, whatever the matter may be.

—Lord Kelvin (1824–1907)

1

What's Wrong With Evaluation?

● ●

In the past two decades, there has been an explosion of evaluation models and theories. Books are being published; conferences are saturated with evaluation presentations. Niche conferences devoted to evaluation take place in the United States, England, Canada, the Netherlands, South Africa, Australia, Japan, and elsewhere. Journals highlight new theories and models, and practitioners take advantage of email distribution lists and online chat rooms to discuss specific evaluation issues.

Yet, in the midst of this hoopla, one fact still remains: Evaluation is not effective in many organizations. Many practitioners are not pleased with the success of their measurement and evaluation systems that involve only reaction-level evaluation, which was introduced formally by Kirkpatrick in the 1950s (Kirkpatrick, 1998). Others concentrate on measuring learning but achieve only mixed results. Few go beyond the classroom or keyboard to measure changes in the workplace linked to learning and development programs. The use of return-on-investment (ROI) calculations for learning and development programs is even rarer. The Corporate Executive Board's study, "Reframing the Measurement Debate" (Drimmer, 2002), shows that although 78 percent of those participating in the study have evaluating ROI on their wish list, only 11 percent are actually evaluating programs using ROI.

This book focuses on making evaluation effective in the organization, whatever the model, process, or theory selected. This first chapter focuses on the problems with evaluation and highlights concerns voiced by many practitioners. In these discussions, there is some hint of how the situation may be improved. Also, this chapter points out particular chapters to help you go straight to the issues most relevant to your own situation and experience.

● ●

Evaluation Problems

Although measures of program success are being used increasingly across private and public sectors, the key question becomes, "Given the pressure to show accountability and results, why aren't organizations doing more?" The barriers to conducting meaningful evaluation are 12 basic problems.

Problem #1: Too Many Theories and Models

Since Kirkpatrick provided his four levels of evaluation in the late 1950s, dozens of evaluation books have been written just for the learning and development community. Add to this the hundreds of evaluation books written primarily for the social sciences, education, and government organizations. Then, add the 100-plus models and theories for evaluation offered to practitioners to help them measure the contribution of learning and development, each claiming a unique approach and a promise of addressing evaluation woes and bringing about world peace.

Some of these models and theories are based on the success or progress in a particular organization. Others are refinements of existing models designed to shore up the weaknesses or fill in the gaps of existing methodology. Still others are developed by professors and researchers who are attempting to find the one best way to evaluate.

Every year, pages of the *Human Resource Development Quarterly, Management Learning, Performance Improvement Quarterly, Human Resource Development Review, Learning and Education, International Journal of Training and Development, Human Resource Development International,* and other respected scholarly and research-based journals offer new models. Often these are the creations of individuals trying to make their mark in the world of evaluation.

Kirkpatrick's four levels of evaluation spawned a plethora of imitators, but many new models are aimed at destroying the four-level framework. The Kirkpatrick framework is repeatedly debated by researchers, yet, it is still the most widely accepted framework by practitioners. Originally, it was not presented as a model to evaluate training. It was offered as a framework of succeeding levels (steps), showing a chain of impact that must exist if the training is to add value. Kirkpatrick did not claim to show how all of this is done, rather he presented a pragmatic approach to categorize data to show the complete success of programs. At a recent learning and development conference, a professor/consultant in the field suggested Kirkpatrick's four levels are dead. Yet, how can a framework be dead if most practitioners are still eagerly pursuing it with much success?

Conferences have offered much information and coverage of the evaluation issue. The largest conference in the field, ASTD's annual International Conference and Exposition, regularly focuses on evaluation through its measurement and evaluation track and now with a special conference-within-a-conference on measurement, evaluation, and ROI. Other conferences are devoted exclusively to this critical topic and offer yet another opportunity for researchers, professors, and practitioners to espouse a new model or theory designed to take care of all of the ills of the previous models.

All this information, activity, and discussion lead many practitioners to appropriately proclaim, "Enough is enough! Stop showing us new models and theories! Focus instead on how to make this work in our organization." Practitioners have several legitimate questions: How can they build on existing and widely adopted processes and make them work in a routine and consistent way? How do they simplify what appears to be a very difficult and challenging issue? How can they implement evaluation and stay within the budget?

Evaluation theorists and researchers face the challenge of convincing practitioners to use their models; practitioners are challenged with sorting out how to use a new model. Although this book does not present new models or theories, it does help organizations work with existing ones. Chapter 4 provides criteria that may be helpful when selecting an appropriate model. The rest of the book is aimed at "How do you make evaluation work in the organization?"

Problem #2: Models Are Too Complex

Evaluation is a difficult issue. Because situations, programs, solutions, and organizations are different, implementing an evaluation process across multiple programs and organizations is quite complex. Many evaluation models have very long formulas designed for specific, narrowly focused situations. Consider, for example, the formula to develop the impact of learning using the concept of utility analysis shown in figure 1-1. This particular process is used to place a value on new skills, disregarding the actual impact of those skills in the workplace. While the approach may be valuable and helpful, it appears to be a daunting task from the practitioner's perspective.

The complexity of evaluation models often stems from the source. Most models are developed by researchers, professors, and practitioners with extensive research backgrounds. Researchers often strive for purity and attempt to address every scenario or situation, resulting in models with many parts, components, and formulas that are often frightening and confusing to those charged with doing something about it.

The challenge is to develop models that are theoretically sound, yet simple and usable. The challenge for practitioners is to apply the simplified models, yet keep the credibility intact. These are achievable goals, but they require building expertise in evaluation and developing an understanding of evaluation models and theories.

Problem #3: Lack of Understanding of Evaluation

Evaluation is not usually part of the preparation for an assignment in learning and development. Even human resource development degree programs do not always include evaluation in their curricula. Building expertise in evaluation takes time. Unfortunately, busy practitioners often do not or will not take the time to learn evaluation. Even if they do, it hasn't always been easy for practitioners to learn this process. Some books on the subject have 600 pages, making it impossible for a practitioner to absorb just through reading.

Until recently, there were few workshops dedicated to evaluation. Now, two-day evaluation workshops are offered 20 to 30 times a year in the United States alone. An evaluation certification process is available that provides practitioners responsible for evaluation an opportunity to learn specific skills (J.J. Phillips, 2003). Also, networks

---

Figure 1-1. An example of a complicated formula.

Utility Analysis

Utility analysis measures the economic contribution of a program according to how effective the program was in identifying and modifying behavior, and hence the future service contribution of employees. The Brogden utility estimation equation (Brodgen, 1946; 1949) can be used to estimate the dollar value of a training program:

$$\overline{\Delta U} = N \times T \times d_t \times SD_y - c$$

where

$\overline{\Delta U}$ = the total change in utility in dollars after the training program
N = number of employees trained
T = duration, in number of years, of a training program's effect on performance
SD_y = standard deviation of job performance of the untrained group in dollars
d_t = true difference in job performance between the average trained and the average untrained employees in units of standard deviation
c = cost of training per employee

---

and learning communities are available to develop expertise and exchange information.

Not only is it essential for the evaluator to understand evaluation processes, but also the entire learning and development staff must learn parts of the process and understand how evaluation fits into their role. To remedy this situation, it is essential for the organization to focus on how expertise is developed and disseminated within the organization. Additional information on this issue is contained in chapter 5.

Problem #4: The Search for Statistical Precision

Evaluation data are intended to provide decision-making information. Decisions may include redesigning, updating, or completely revamping a learning and development program. The decision could even be to do nothing because the program is very effective. At the other extreme, evaluation data could lead to abandoning a program. In terms of new programs, evaluation data is collected during a pilot project to decide whether the program should be implemented throughout the organization.

Historically, such decisions were based primarily on reaction/feedback data generated as individuals observed, viewed, or participated in the learning solution. A more appropriate approach is to obtain data beyond reactive feedback. Data showing what individuals are learning, how skills and knowledge are being applied, and the value the program adds to the organization provides a solid basis for decision making.

Ultimately, the statistical analysis issue arises in these situations. Some researchers and experts suggest that statistical precision be brought to the analysis process and that decisions be made at the 95 percent confidence level, a statistical concept for accuracy. Although this may be ideal, problems usually surface in practice. Often the reality of the workplace dictates that decisions be made with less-than-statistically-sound data.

An example illustrates this issue. In a retail store chain of 420 stores, a pilot learning program on interactive selling skills is implemented in three stores. Based on the results in three stores, the decision is made to implement the program in the other locations. The program shows significant impact as the evaluation generates several types of data including the actual ROI (Phillips & Phillips, 2001). A question quickly emerges, "Can we assume that the other 417 stores will have the same results as the three stores in the pilot group?" Clearly, the answer is no. It would take a sample of more than 200 stores in the pilot group to be able to make an inference about the success in remaining stores. From a practical basis, this would be impossible and would not be recommended by any individual concerned about the economics of new program implementation.

Statistical accuracy must be balanced with the realities of the workplace. If not, many models and theories would be dead on arrival. Figure 1-2 shows the tradeoff between statistical precision and the cost of getting to that level of accuracy. The challenge is to locate an acceptable range of costs and accuracy.

In many cases, there is a desire for lower evaluation costs, thereby lowering the level of accuracy. This news is not all bad. Evaluation models available today are bringing together more objective data than was available in the past. Also, there is growing evidence that extensive analysis and precision are unnecessary and sometimes even inhibit performance (Sutcliffe & Weber, 2003). Decision making today is based on richer and more balanced data than used previously.

So, when should statistical precision be pursued? The answer is that statistical precision is needed when a high-stakes decision is being made and when plenty of time and resources are available.

Problem #5: Evaluation Is Considered a Post-Program Activity

Most evaluation is developed as an after-the-fact process; after everything is completed, a check is done to see if it was successful. Therefore, from the beginning, most evaluation was entirely reactive,

Figure 1-2. The tradeoff between accuracy and cost.

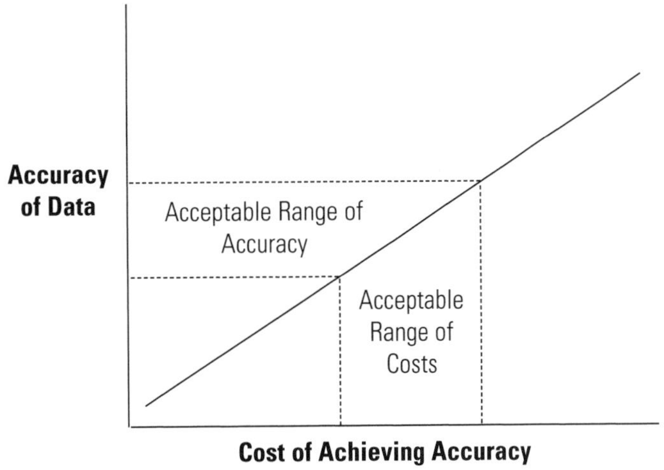

based on someone's request, after the program had been implemented.

The most appropriate way to use evaluation, though, is to consider the process up front, prior to program development. When you take this approach, you can conduct evaluation efficiently and enhance the quality and quantity of data you collect. You can clearly define specific measures, secure commitment from those who should provide specific data, and use various techniques to ensure that data is collected properly, effectively, and efficiently.

Ideally, the evaluation strategy should be developed after the needs assessment is conducted. As specific objectives are defined, the basis for the evaluation is determined. This approach enhances the likelihood of having an acceptable quality and quantity of data throughout the process.

In some cases, evaluators must forecast the value of a program before it is designed, developed, or delivered. Through the follow-up process, the post-program data can be compared to forecast data to determine how well forecasting is working. Therefore, forecasting is an important tool in the evaluation model.

In short, evaluation is not a post-program activity but is an activity that must be considered early and often in the process to enhance its efficiency and effectiveness for collecting data and making decisions.

Problem #6: Failure to See the Long-Term Payoff of Evaluation

Evaluation is often implemented for narrowly focused reasons. Consequently, the big picture is often missed. Evaluation not only improves individual programs and solutions, but also the entire learning and development function. Some learning and development executives have indicated that a comprehensive measurement and evaluation process has caused them to reinvent learning and development to align those activities with business needs, focus on accountability, meet customer requirements and needs, and produce results desired by the senior leadership in the organization.

Developing the long-term payoff of evaluation requires examining multiple rationales for pursuing evaluation. Evaluation can be used to

- determine success in achieving program objectives
- identify the strengths and weaknesses in the learning and development process
- prioritize resources for learning and development
- enhance the accountability of learning and development
- compare the benefits to the costs of a learning and development program

- decide who should participate in future programs
- test the clarity and validity of tests, cases, and exercises
- identify the participants who were the most (and least) successful with the program
- reinforce major points made during the program
- improve the quality of learning and development
- assist in marketing future programs
- determine if the program was an appropriate solution for the specific need
- establish a database to assist management in decision making.

Most important, however, evaluators should consider evaluation as a process improvement tool to make learning and development more effective and aligned with the organization.

Problem #7: Lack of Support From Key Stakeholders

Some implementations of evaluation models have failed because the key stakeholders did not support them fully. The number, variety, and specific roles of stakeholders have increased in recent years. For example, figure 1-3 shows a list of the key stakeholders in Saturn University (Wall & White, 1997).

Although a measurement specialist has primary responsibility for evaluation, other stakeholders have roles in the evaluation process and must understand what evaluation will do for them as well as what it will do for the organization. Otherwise, they may fear or resist the outcome.

Specific steps must be taken to win support and buy-in from key groups including senior executives and the management group. Executives must see that evaluation produces valuable data to improve processes and programs. Managers of specific learners often want to know if the time invested will pay off for them in their business units and add value directly to their departments and functions. Participants often want to know what is in it for them as they provide reaction or performance data. The learning and development staff must view evaluation as a process improvement tool and not a performance evaluation tool. They must be convinced that this evaluation data will not be used to reflect unfavorably on their own individual performance. When the stakeholders understand what's involved, they will be more likely to offer their support.

Sometimes evaluation is confused with auditing. If evaluators ask unannounced for all types of data that the participants or others are not anticipating, the results will likely be unsatisfactory. A more productive approach is to build expectations

Figure 1-3. Stakeholders in learning and development at Saturn University.

Leader
- Saturn Action Council
- Other Leader
- Training Coordinator
- Manufacturing Training Leader
- Team

Trainer
- People Systems Training and Development
- Course Owner
- Developer
- Trainer
- Training Point Person
- Measurement Specialist

Source: Wall, S., and E. White. (1997). "Building Saturn's Organization-wide Transfer Support Model." In: M. Broad (editor) and J.J. Phillips (series editor), *In Action: Transferring Learning to the Workplace.* Alexandria, VA: ASTD. Adapted with permission.

so that individuals willingly provide the required data at the right time. This approach will probably yield sufficient quantities of high-quality data to conduct meaningful evaluation. Furthermore, stakeholders will be more likely to actually use the results of evaluation.

Problem #8: Evaluation Hasn't Delivered the Data Senior Managers Want

Although many stakeholders are involved in learning and development, there are two major customer groups. The first group encompasses those involved directly in the programs, often labeled the consumers of the process. The other important group is the client group—the individuals who sponsor, approve, or initiate major programs. These people are often the senior management team.

Previously, most evaluation data was collected to satisfy needs of the consumers. Evaluators used reaction data representing feedback from consumers to make programs and solutions more palatable to the consumers. The learning data was often fed back to consumers so that they were aware of their knowledge acquisition or skill enhancement. This feedback helped build confidence in using skills and knowledge in the program.

Today, clients are asking for data beyond reaction and learning. They need data on the application of new skills on the job and the corresponding impact in the business units. Sometimes they want ROI data for major programs. They request data to show the business impact of learning and development both from a short-term and a long-term perspective. This requirement represents a major shift, and some evaluation models have failed to deliver adequate data, particularly in regard to business impact and ROI.

Any model or process that does not provide data needed by the senior management group is destined to fail in the organization. Ultimately, these executives are the ones who must continue funding learning and development. If the desired data is not available, future funding could be in jeopardy.

Problem #9: Improper Use of Evaluation Data

As Mark Twain once said, "Collecting data is like collecting garbage. Pretty soon, we have to do something with it." If not used properly, evaluation data is useless. Improper use of evaluation data can lead to four major problems:

1. Too many organizations do not use evaluation data at all. In these situations, data is collected, tabulated, catalogued, filed, and never used by any particular group other than the individual who initially collected the data.

2. Data is not provided to the appropriate groups. Different groups need different types of data and often in very different formats. Analyzing the target audiences and determining the specific data needed for each group are important for communicating data.

3. Data is not used to drive improvement. Most evaluation data uncovers process improvement opportunities and identifies features that could be adjusted or changes that should be made to make the program more effective. If not part of the feedback cycle, evaluation falls short of what it is intended to do.

4. Data is used for the wrong reasons—to take action against an individual or group or to withhold funds rather than improving processes. Sometimes the data is used in very political ways to gain power or advantage over another person.

These problems represent dysfunctional activities that can destroy evaluation processes. They must be addressed if evaluation is to add value. Chapter 6 shows how evaluation data can be communicated and should be used to drive action in the organization.

Problem #10: Inconsistency

For evaluation to add value and be accepted by different stakeholders, it must be consistent in its approach and methodology. Tools and templates need to be developed to support the method of choice to prevent perpetual reinvention of the wheel. The evaluation process should be systematic and follow step-by-step procedures. When possible, evaluation should be built in so that it becomes a seamless part of the learning and development process. Evaluation procedures must be consistent from one project to another. Without consistency, evaluation consumes too many resources and raises too many concerns about the quality of the process.

Problem #11: A Lack of Standards

Closely paralleled with consistency is the issue of standards. Standards are rules for making evaluation consistent, stable, and equitable. Without standards, there is little consistency in processes and stability in outcomes. Evaluation standards are needed to set minimum levels of coverage for steps, processes, and techniques, and to reflect acceptable practices. Standards need to be developed for data collection, cost calculations, data analysis, interpretation, and communications. Standards should be based on best practices that are feasible within specific settings. Standards show how the concepts of accuracy and the use of statistics are integrated into evaluation to build needed credibility, and, at the same time, suggest ways in which the process can be conducted in an economically feasible way.

Problem #12: Sustainability

Sustainability refers to integrating evaluation into the organization so that it becomes routine. Unfortunately, most organizations have not been able to sustain the same evaluation process for a long period of time. To accomplish this, the evaluation process must gain respect of key stakeholders at the outset. The evaluation process must be well documented, and stakeholders must accept their responsibilities to make it work. Without sustainability, evaluation will be on a roller-coaster ride in which proper attention is focused on programs only when they are in trouble and less attention is given to them when they are not. This continual up-and-down cycle in terms of equipment, tools, and funding is a waste of talent and resources, not to mention a lost opportunity to improve processes and programs. Evaluation must be implemented, refined, improved, and maintained for the long term. Chapter 9 shows how to make evaluation routine.

Final Thoughts

This chapter presents the major evaluation problems that practitioners have experienced in the past two decades of implementation. Most of the chapters in this book will illustrate how these problems can be prevented, overcome, or even eliminated as evaluation becomes an ongoing routine and successful part of the organization.

2

Evaluation Myths
and Mysteries

• •

Practitioners recognize that additional measurement and evaluation is needed; however, they struggle with how to address the issue, regardless of the motivation to pursue evaluation. They often ask, "Does it provide the benefits to make it a routine useful tool?" "Is it feasible within our resources?" "Do we have the capability of implementing a comprehensive evaluation process?" The answers to these questions often lead to debate and even controversy. Controversy stems from misunderstandings about what the additional evaluation can and cannot do and how it can or should be implemented in organizations. This chapter explores misunderstandings surrounding measurement and evaluation.

• •

The Myths of Measurement and Evaluation

Exercise 2-1 presents a list of 15 issues (or myths) most often debated with regard to measurement and evaluation. Before reading further, check each statement in the table to indicate whether the issue is myth or reality.

Myth #1: Measurement and Evaluation Is Too Expensive

Cost is usually the first issue to surface when considering additional measurement and evaluation. Many practitioners see evaluation adding cost to an already lean budget that is regularly scrutinized. Even if the cost is relatively small, practitioners often rationalize that they cannot afford additional measurement and evaluation.

This rationalization is often based on myths. When the cost of evaluation is compared to the budget, a comprehensive measurement and evaluation system can be implemented for less than 5 percent of the total direct learning and development budget. Best practice organizations often spend 3 to 5 percent of the direct training budget on measurement and evaluation. Some organizations can do it with less (Burkett, 2001).

The issues around this myth are often concerned with the cost of detailed impact studies versus routine evaluation. Detailed impact studies should be conducted only for programs that are very expensive or highly strategic or involve many different individuals. In a recent survey of 2,189 public sector training and HR professionals representing federal, state, and local agencies, the 523 respondents indicated

---

Exercise 2-1. Myth or reality? You decide.

Check each item indicating whether you perceive the issue to be myth or reality.

	Myth	Reality
1. Measurement and evaluation is too expensive.	☐	☐
2. Evaluation takes too much time.	☐	☐
3. If senior management does not require additional measurement, there is no need to pursue it.	☐	☐
4. Measurement and evaluation is a passing fad.	☐	☐
5. Evaluation generates only one or two types of data.	☐	☐
6. Evaluation cannot be easily replicated.	☐	☐
7. Evaluation is too subjective.	☐	☐
8. Impact evaluation is not possible for soft skills programs, only for technical and hard skills programs.	☐	☐
9. Evaluation is more appropriate for certain types of organizations.	☐	☐
10. It is not always possible to isolate the effects of learning and development.	☐	☐
11. Because learning and development staff have no control over participants after they complete a program, evaluating the on-the-job improvement is not appropriate.	☐	☐
12. A participant is rarely responsible for the failure of programs.	☐	☐
13. Evaluation is only the evaluator's responsibility.	☐	☐
14. Successful evaluation implementation requires a university degree in statistics or evaluation.	☐	☐
15. Negative data is always bad news.	☐	☐

Although each issue appears to be valid, they are all myths. Each of these issues can be addressed and overcome through careful planning and a thorough understanding of the evaluation process. The remainder of this chapter elaborates on each issue, explaining the reality behind the myth.

criteria necessary to evaluate programs at higher levels, including ROI (P.P. Phillips, 2003). These criteria include programs that are aligned with organization strategy, are linked to operational goals, are expensive, or are associated with a high degree of management interest.

Other programs do not need extensive evaluation. In many cases, reaction and learning data is sufficient. The challenge is to understand when and how to be comprehensive. When it is necessary to embark on detailed impact studies, a variety of cost-saving techniques can be used, including software, templates, estimates, guidelines, and sharing responsibilities. These techniques ensure that evaluation does not consume excessive resources.

Myth #2: Evaluation Takes Too Much Time

Parallel with the concern about cost is the actual time involved in evaluation—time to design evaluation instruments, collect data, process the data, and communicate results to a variety of groups. Selecting programs carefully for comprehensive evaluations and assigning the necessary activities for them among different groups will save time. Building in processes and automated techniques and templates as well as streamlining communications can also reduce the time commitment. Dozens of shortcuts are available to help reduce the total time requirements for evaluation (Phillips & Burkett, 2001).

The important point is to consider the alternative. If the proper amount of time is not taken, the consequences may be more serious. When prioritizing time commitments, there may be more value in allocating time to evaluation than to creating, revising, and implementing programs that are unnecessary or are not working.

Myth #3: If Senior Management Does Not Require Additional Measurement, There Is No Need to Pursue It

This myth captures the most innocent bystanders. Its premise lulls practitioners into providing to senior management activity-related data that simply meets the status quo. The assumption is that no pressure or requests equate to no requirement for more meaningful data.

The early approaches to evaluation focused on presenting indicator data and disguising it as results. Examples of indicator data include the number of programs, number of participants, number of hours, the costs, and the topics on which employees are trained. These indicators represent the "investment" made by the organization to train and develop employees. Practitioners often think that indicator data is what executives want because they haven't asked for anything else. Continuously reporting indicator data only leaves the learning and development function at risk. When organizations downsize, this function is sometimes the first group to go.

Sometimes senior executives fail to ask for outcome data because they think that it is not available. They may assume that it cannot be produced. There is another danger in believing this myth. Paradigms are shifting, not only within learning and development context, but within senior management groups as well. Senior managers *are* beginning to request higher level data that shows application, impact, and even ROI. In a recent management meeting, a senior executive proclaimed, "It's not what they learn, it's what they do with what they learn that is important." Changes in corporate leadership sometimes initiate important paradigm shifts. New leadership often requires evidence of accountability. If there is no evidence of results, the learning and development function becomes an easy target for staff reductions. When senior executives suddenly ask for results, they expect a quick response. The process of integrating additional measurement in an organization takes time. It is not a quick fix. Because of this, the learning and development staff must initiate additional measurement and evaluation long before results are requested.

Myth #4: Measurement and Evaluation Is a Passing Fad

Unfortunately, some practitioners regard the move to more evaluation as another passing fad, a "flavor of the month" that will soon go away. The critical question becomes, "Will this, too, pass?" Accountability is a concern now. Many organizations are being asked to show the value of programs.

Unfortunately, accountability for expenditures and concern about the value of programs are always issues. Many evaluation processes can show the ultimate level of accountability, which is the cost versus the benefits. Although in recent years more focus has been placed on accountability, including ROI, the need for sound measurement and evaluation has always existed. The need continues to grow as organizations' budgets increase and as the learning and development function competes with other parts of the organization for resources. Even ROI will continue to be an important tool to show the impact of learning and development programs.

Myth #5: Evaluation Generates Only One or Two Types of Data

Although some evaluation processes generate a single type of data (reaction-level data, for example),

many evaluation models and processes generate a variety of data, offering a balanced approach based on both qualitative and quantitative data. As shown in table 2-1, some models generate as many as six different types of qualitative and quantitative data collected at different timeframes and from different sources (Phillips & Stone, 2002). The data can be as rich and comprehensive as necessary to make important decisions and drive improvements in learning and development programs.

Myth #6: Evaluation Cannot Be Easily Replicated

With so many different evaluation processes available, this issue becomes an understandable concern. In theory, any process worthy of implementation is one that can be replicated from one study to another. For example, two different people should be able to evaluate the same learning and development program and obtain the same results. If they cannot, the process is flawed, leaving the results dependent on the individual conducting the study.

Table 2-1. Types of evaluation data.

Types of Data	Definition	Focus
Reaction and Planned Action	Measures participant satisfaction with the program and captures planned actions, if appropriate	Focus is on the learning program, the facilitator, and how application might occur.
Learning	Measures changes in knowledge, skills, and attitudes	Focus is on the participant and various support mechanisms for learning.
Application	Measures changes in on-the-job behavior or actions as the program is applied, implemented, or utilized	Focus is on the participant, the work setting, and support mechanisms for applying learning.
Business Impact	Measures changes in business impact data	Focus is on the impact of learning on specific organizational outcomes.
Return-on-Investment	Compares program benefits to the cost of the program	Focus is on the monetary benefits derived from the learning program.
Intangible Benefits	Refers to measures that are not converted to monetary benefits	Focus is on the added value of learning in nonmonetary terms.

Source: Adapted from Phillips, J.J., and R.D. Stone. (2002). *How to Measure Training Results: A Practical Guide for Tracking the Six Key Indicators.* New York: McGraw-Hill.

Fortunately, many evaluation models offer a systematic process with certain guiding principles or operating standards to increase the likelihood that two different evaluators will obtain the same results. Figure 2-1 shows the guiding principles for one popular evaluation model.

Myth #7: Evaluation Is Too Subjective

Subjectivity of evaluation has become a concern in part because of the number of studies conducted using estimates that have been published and presented at conferences. The fact is that many studies are precise and are not based on estimates. Problems with estimates often surface when attempting to isolate the effects of other factors. Estimates represent only one of the many techniques available to isolate the effects of programs on output data. Other techniques use analytical approaches, such as control groups, time series analysis, and regression equations. Estimates are used when no other technique will work.

Sometimes evaluators use estimates when converting data to monetary value or estimating output in the data collection phase. Although estimates may represent the worst case scenario in evaluation, they can be extremely reliable when they are obtained carefully, adjusted for error, and reported appropriately. The accounting, engineering, and technology fields routinely use estimates, often without question or concern. This should be the case for evaluation of learning and development as well. Subjectivity can be managed— even when estimates are used.

Myth #8: Impact Evaluation Is Not Possible for Soft Skills Programs, Only for Technical and Hard Skills Programs

This assumption is often based on the concern that soft skills programs are sometimes difficult to measure. Practitioners have a problem understanding how to measure the success of leadership, team-building, and communication programs, for example. What they often misunderstand is that soft skills learning and development programs can drive such hard data items as output, quality, cost, and time.

Case after case shows successful evaluation of programs using soft skills that are linked directly to hard data items. Figure 2-2 demonstrates how a soft skills program on leadership development can lead to hard data items that can be converted to monetary value when an ROI calculation is necessary.

Figure 2-1. Examples of operating standards for an evaluation methodology.

Guiding Principles

1. When a higher-level evaluation is conducted, data must be collected at lower levels.
2. When an evaluation is planned for a higher-level, the previous level of evaluation does not have to be comprehensive.
3. When collecting and analyzing data, use only the most credible source.
4. When analyzing data, choose the most conservative among the alternatives.
5. At least one method must be used to isolate the effects of the solution.
6. If no improvement data is available for a population or from a specific source, it is assumed that little or no improvement has occurred.
7. Estimates of improvements should be adjusted (discounted) for the potential error of the estimate.
8. Extreme data items and unsupported claims should not be used in the ROI analysis of short-term solutions.
9. Only the first year of benefits (annual) should be used in the ROI analysis of short-term solutions.
10. Costs of the solution should be fully loaded for ROI analysis.
11. Intangible measures are defined as measures that are purposely not converted to monetary values.
12. The results from the ROI Methodology must be communicated to all key stakeholders

---

Source: Adapted from Phillips, J.J. (2003). *Return on Investment in Training and Performance Improvement Programs,* 2nd edition. Boston: Butterworth-Heinemann.

Figure 2-2. Soft skills learning leads to hard data outputs.

		Productive Teams	Leads to → Increased Output	= Time Savings
		Employee Satisfaction	Leads to → Reduced Turnover	= Reduced Costs
Leadership Development	Leads to →	Quality Products	Leads to → Fewer Returns	= Reduced Costs
		Revenue Generation	Leads to → Increased Profits	= Increased profits
		Reduced Cycle Time	Leads to → Time Saving	= Reduced Costs

Impact and ROI analysis are conducted more often with soft skills programs than hard skills programs.

The confusion intensifies when soft skills programs are implemented without a linkage to a particular business need. When there is no business need, it is difficult to connect the application of the soft skills to a business measure. Consequently, there are no results. This issue challenges even the most sophisticated organizations. The key issue is to ensure that the front-end analysis is conducted so that the program is connected to a business measure.

Myth #9: Evaluation Is More Appropriate for Certain Types of Organizations

Although evaluation is easier in certain types of programs, generally, evaluation can be used in any setting. Comprehensive measurement systems are successfully implemented in health care, nonprofit, government, and educational areas in addition to traditional service and manufacturing organizations. Regardless of the type of organization, there is a need to know the success of learning and development programs. Sometimes success is measured in terms of impact for a particular group. Impact data, whether hard or soft, is converted into measures representing output, quality, cost, time, and satisfaction. These measures exist in all organizations.

Another concern expressed by some is that only large organizations have a need for measurement and

evaluation. Although this may appear to be the case (because large organizations have large budgets), in reality, evaluation can work in the smallest organizations; it just has to be scaled down to fit the situation. Even firms with as few as 40 employees have implemented a comprehensive evaluation to show the success of learning programs (Devany, 2001).

Myth #10: It Is Not Always Possible to Isolate the Effects of Learning and Development

Isolating the effects of learning and development programs from other factors affecting the organization is a difficult issue. For example, how can you know for sure that an improvement in a key business measure is due to a learning and development program and not due to, say, a new customer-tracking program in the sales department?

Several methods are available to isolate the effects of a given program or intervention. The challenge is to select an appropriate isolation technique for the resources available and the accuracy needed in the particular situation.

Excluding the isolation step makes it impossible to know the linkage between the learning program and key business measures. In some cases, not knowing the linkage makes it seem as if the learning and development program isn't contributing to the organization's bottom line; in other cases, it seems that learning and development is taking complete credit for particular outcomes, ignoring other influences. Ignoring the issue of isolation leaves the impression that the learning and development staff does not know how to tackle the issue. The consequences can be disastrous.

This myth stems from unsuccessful attempts to use a control group arrangement, a classic way of isolating the effects of a learning and development program. In practice, a control group does not work in the majority of situations, causing some researchers to abandon the issue. In reality, other techniques such as trend line analysis, forecasting, and expert estimation are accurate, reliable, and valid methods for isolation.

Myth #11: Because Learning and Development Staff Have No Control Over Participants After They Complete a Program, Evaluating the On-the-Job Improvement Is Not Appropriate

This myth is based on the assumption that the learning and development staff lose influence after the program is completed. This is not (or should not be) the case. This myth is fading as organizations realize the importance of measuring results of workplace solutions. Systems and processes can be implemented to influence application. Expectations can be created so that participants anticipate a follow-up.

Although the learning and development staff does not have direct control over what happens in the workplace, it does have influence on the learning transfer process. A learning and development program is owned by the organization, not necessarily the learning and development department. Many individuals and groups are (or should be) involved in a learning program. All stakeholders have some responsibility for success. Objectives are developed to push expectations beyond the classroom and the keyboard. Objectives focus not only on what participants will learn, but also on what they are expected to do with what they learned and the expected consequence of applying what they learned. A partnership is needed between key managers and the

learning and development staff. The learning and development staff must accept responsibility for success or failure beyond the classroom or keyboard and explore ways to make sure learning transfers to the workplace.

Myth #12: A Participant Is Rarely Responsible for the Failure of Programs

When learning and development programs fail, one of two groups are routinely blamed. Usually the failure is pinned on the learning and development staff for ineffective design, delivery, or content. Sometimes, the managers are blamed because they do not support the learning and development program. Although these are two likely culprits, sometimes the real problem is the participants. Too often participants are allowed to escape accountability for their learning experience. It is too easy for participants to claim that the program was not supported by their manager or that it did not fit the culture of the work group, or that the systems or processes are in conflict with the skills and processes taught in the program.

Today, participants are being held more accountable for success of learning. Traditionally, they have only been asked to participate in learning and development opportunities to learn and then apply new skills and knowledge. This is fundamental. The new twist is that participants not only have responsibility to apply what they learn but to achieve results as well. Also, they are asked to provide data to show the success of their program. This creates expectations—and sometimes pressure—on participants to achieve meaningful results. Sometimes they are prepared to analyze barriers and determine ways to circumvent the barriers or minimize their effect on application of skills. Evaluators ask participants to examine the actual consequences of their learning and detail the actual business impact and sometimes calculate its economic value. This challenge helps participants view learning and development programs with results-based expectations rather than activity-based expectations. Communicating this important issue is a critical step toward developing results-based programs.

Myth #13: Evaluation Is Only the Evaluator's Responsibility

Some organizations assign an individual or group primary responsibility for evaluation. Other stakeholders assume that they have no responsibility for evaluation. In today's climate, evaluation must be a shared responsibility. All stakeholders are involved in some aspect of analyzing, designing, developing, delivering, implementing, coordinating, or organizing a learning program. Managers and participants provide information on performance and skills deficits. Learning team members design, develop, and deliver the program. In the process, the evaluation plan is developed. Decisions are made about data collection and analysis. Managers and key stakeholders provide input to the plan. Buy-in is obtained from senior management. After the program, participants and managers provide data. Evaluation is the responsibility of all stakeholders.

Myth #14: Successful Evaluation Implementation Requires a University Degree in Statistics or Evaluation

Some individuals fear evaluation. They fear data and numbers and mathematics and statistics. They assume that special training is needed to tackle evaluation in an organization. They assume that a degree in mathematics, statistics, psychology, or evaluation is a prerequisite to conducing successful evaluation.

In reality, it is not a requirement to hold a degree or possess some special skill or knowledge. Eagerness to learn, willingness to analyze data, and a desire to make improvements in the organization are primary requirements. With these requirements met, most individuals can learn how to properly implement evaluation. Many evaluation models and practices do not necessarily require statistics. Even when they do, the techniques and routines are often basic and fundamental, at least for the more widely used and acceptable models.

This myth is sometimes perpetuated because most evaluation models and theories are developed by individuals with doctoral degrees and are often more complex than they need to be. Attempting to simplify the complicated processes is a challenge facing many practitioners. The most successful evaluation processes are those that are credible, yet simple, in which the practitioner can conduct the evaluation and can explain the process to key managers so that they can understand it.

Myth #15: Negative Data Is Always Bad News

Negative data (defined as data that is below expectations) can appear in many ways. Data may reveal that the reaction to the program is inadequate, the levels of learning are unacceptable, learners have not applied skills and knowledge on the job, business impact fell short of expectations, or that the ROI itself is negative or less than expected.

Although these may be less-than-desired outcomes, negative data provides a rich source of information for improvement. An effective evaluation system can pinpoint what went wrong so that changes can be made. An effective evaluation system can identify barriers to success as well as enablers of success. It will generate conclusions that show what must be changed to make the process more effective. The critical issue around this myth is the misuse of the negative data. If negative data is used to criticize and punish those who are involved, then negative data is indeed bad news. But, an effective evaluation system built on process improvement takes negative data and uses it as the basis for improvement.

Final Thoughts

This chapter explored 15 myths about evaluation. As with all myths, they are based on false perceptions or misunderstandings. These myths inhibit successful evaluation in many organizations. They must be confronted, eliminated, or minimized. Chapters throughout the book focus on how to overcome these myths.

3

The Payoff of Investing in Measurement and Evaluation

Whenever a new program is implemented, one question always crops up: "What's the payoff?" Although some payoffs are obvious, the advantages of investing time and resources in measurement and evaluation vary. This chapter itemizes 15 potential payoffs for investing in measurement and evaluation.

What's the Payoff?

You might find it helpful to examine the payoffs listed in exercise 3-1 to help you assess the potential payoff of your approach to evaluation.

Payoff #1: Response, Requests, and Requirements

In today's competitive environment, many CEOs, top executives, administrators, and clients require additional data beyond the traditional measurement of reaction and learning. Today's executives and administrators need information about application and implementation in the workplace and the corresponding impact on key business measures. In some cases, they are asking for ROI analysis.

To meet these needs, organizations must go beyond their present measurement and evaluation processes and invest in tools that provide insight into measures required by senior management. Developing a comprehensive measurement and evaluation system is the best strategy to meet these requests and requirements. To ignore a request for more evaluation data is inappropriate, unnecessary, and in some cases risky—the consequences are great. Responding to requests and requirements of top executives and administrators is necessary and often results in very positive consequences. A comprehensive measurement and evaluation process can have long-term payoffs.

Payoff #2: Budget Justification

The need to invest additional funds into measurement and evaluation is sometimes based on reaction to budget concerns. Evaluation data may be necessary to show the value of an existing learning and development budget allocated to convince executives that programs are effective. Some learning and development functions use additional evaluation data to support a requested budget. It is not unusual for budget requests to be reviewed in light of the

---

Exercise 3-1. Payoff of current evaluation system.

Does your approach to evaluation result in the following payoffs?

	Yes	No
1. Response, requests, and requirements	☐	☐
2. Budget justification	☐	☐
3. Improve program design	☐	☐
4. Identify and improve dysfunctional processes	☐	☐
5. Enhance the transfer of learning	☐	☐
6. Eliminate unnecessary or ineffective programs	☐	☐
7. Expand or implement successful programs	☐	☐
8. Enhance the respect and credibility of the learning and development staff	☐	☐
9. Satisfy client needs	☐	☐
10. Build support from managers	☐	☐
11. Strengthen relationships with key executives and administrators	☐	☐
12. Set priorities for learning and development	☐	☐
13. Reinvent learning and development	☐	☐
14. Alter management's perceptions of learning and development	☐	☐
15. Achieve a monetary payoff	☐	☐

Although each payoff is possible, many current processes fall short of achieving them. Each of these payoffs can be achieved through careful planning and implementation of evaluation processes. The remainder of this chapter elaborates on how to achieve these payoffs.

value funding brings to the organization. Some learning and development team members use measurement and evaluation to prevent the budget from being slashed, or—in drastic cases—eliminated entirely. Additional evaluation data can show where learning and development programs add value and where they do not. This approach can lead to protecting programs as well as pursuing new programs.

Payoff #3: Improve Program Design

A comprehensive evaluation system should provide information to improve the overall design of a program, including the critical areas of learning design, content, delivery method, duration, timing, focus, and expectations. These processes may need to be adjusted to improve learning, especially during implementation of a new program.

Payoff #4: Identify and Improve Dysfunctional Processes

As with any learning and development implementation, some steps in the learning cycle might have been inadequately addressed or misaligned. The most obvious misstep is the upfront analysis, the traditional training needs assessment, or the performance assessment and analysis.

An evaluation can determine whether the upfront analysis was conducted properly, thereby aligning the program with the organizational needs. Additional measurement and evaluation can also indicate whether interventions are needed other than learning and development. Quite often, organizations initiate learning and development programs to address problems that would be better tackled with other interventions. An effective evaluation system can uncover this situation. It can also uncover unsupportive job environments that may be hindering the use of the learning in the workplace. Effective evaluation can also highlight supportive work environments that enable learning transfer. Finally, effective evaluation can help pinpoint inadequacies in the implementation systems and identify ways to improve these systems.

Payoff #5: Enhance the Transfer of Learning

Closely related to the identification of dysfunctional processes is the enhancement of the transfer of learning to the workplace. Learning transfer is perhaps one of the biggest challenges facing the learning and development field. Research shows that 60 to 90 percent of job-related skills and knowledge acquired in a program still are not being implemented on the job.

Evaluation can play a key role in anticipating, identifying, and mitigating barriers that may block transfer. A comprehensive evaluation system can identify specific individuals that may be blocking or hindering the use of learning. It can shed light on how these barriers can be minimized, reduced, or eliminated altogether so that learning is effectively utilized on the job. Evaluation also identifies people and processes that support the use of skills, so that more attention can be placed on them.

Payoff #6: Eliminate Unnecessary or Ineffective Programs

If a program cannot be redesigned or enhanced so that it adds value, it may be best to discontinue it. Evaluation processes can provide rational, credible data to help make this critical decision. This issue is particularly important when implementing pilot programs. Based on the evaluation data, the decision is made to either implement the program or discontinue it. In reality, if the program does not add the expected value, then it should be discontinued.

One caveat: Eliminating programs should not be a principal motive or rationale for increasing evaluation efforts. Although it is a valid use of evaluation data, program elimination is often viewed more negatively than positively.

Payoff #7: Expand or Implement Successful Programs

The flipside of eliminating programs is expanding their presence or application. Positive evaluation results may signal the possibility that a program's success in one division can be replicated in another division if a similar need exists. Historically, pilot programs were evaluated on subjective and reaction data. Ideally they should be evaluated with application and impact data including ROI calculations in some situations. This payoff for investing in measurement and evaluation can have a huge effect. If a program adds value and is implemented on a wide scale, the contribution can be tremendous, adding value to the entire organization.

Payoff #8: Enhance the Respect and Credibility of the Learning and Development Staff

In too many cases, the credibility of the learning and development function comes into question. Learning and development is sometimes perceived as a process that focuses on satisfaction and morale, making people feel good. Programs are often labeled as fun-and-games activities. It is important to change this perception and build respect for the contribution learning and development bring to the organization. This can be accomplished through a comprehensive measurement and evaluation process. Collecting and using evaluation data—including application, impact, and ROI data—builds respect for learning and respect for the learning and development staff. Appropriate evaluation data enhances the credibility of the learning and development function when the data reveals the value added to the organization.

Payoff #9: Satisfy Client Needs

The client is the individual or group of individuals who fund the learning and development program. The client is involved in initiating or approving programs and often requires additional data to justify support of the learning and development program. In many cases the client wants information about application, implementation, behavior change, and the impact on the business unit. Sometimes clients are interested in the monetary impact of their program investment, including ROI.

Satisfying clients is a critical challenge. If the client is not pleased with the data, he or she may decline the opportunity to use the learning function in the future. If the client is satisfied, he or she may repeat the use of learning as a performance improvement process and even recommend it to others. Client satisfaction is a very important.

Payoff #10: Build Support From Managers

The immediate managers of participants (the supervisors of those attending programs) need convincing data about the success of learning and development activities. They often do not support these processes because they see little value in taking employees off the job to attend a program in which little connection to their business unit is evident. In fact, they often view these activities as a negative impact to their business unit. Data showing how learning and development help them achieve their objectives will influence their support. When they are convinced that learning and development programs are successful, they reinforce learning in the work environment. The payoff of responding to this particular group can be tremendous.

Payoff #11: Strengthen Relationships With Key Executives and Administrators

No group is more important to the learning and development function than senior executives. They allocate funds, commit resources, and show support for the learning and development function in a variety of ways. They must perceive the learning and development function as a business partner that they can invite to the table for important decisions and meetings. A comprehensive measurement process can show the contribution of the learning and development function and help strengthen this relationship. When the learning and development staff is perceived as a business partner, their payoff lies in the influence they can have on the organization.

Payoff #12: Set Priorities for Learning and Development

In almost all organizations, the needs for learning and development exceed the resources available to meet them. A comprehensive measurement system can help determine which programs and projects represent the highest priority. Evaluation data can show the payoff or potential payoff of important and expensive programs.

Armed with this data, the learning and development staff can establish priorities. Programs with highest impact (or potential impact) are often the top priority. Of course, this approach has to be moderated by taking a long view, ensuring that developmental efforts are in place for a long-term payoff. Also, some programs are necessary and represent commitments by the organization. Those concerns aside, the programs with highest priority should be those generating the greatest impact or potential for impact. This can only be achieved with the implementation of a comprehensive measurement system.

Payoff #13: Reinvent Learning and Development

The long-term payoff for investing in measurement and evaluation is the transformation of the learning and development function. Measurement and evaluation reveal the extent of alignment between learning and development and the business, driving increased alignment in the future. This alignment requires a continuous focus on critical organizational needs and results that can and should be obtained from programs and projects. Evaluation data streamlines programs that are inefficient and eliminates those that cannot add value. In essence, evaluation revitalizes, reenergizes, and realigns the learning and development function so that it is a productive part of the organization.

Payoff #14: Alter Management's Perceptions of Learning and Development

This important payoff focuses on the middle-level managers who often question the value of learning and development. They often see learning and development as a necessary evil. A comprehensive evaluation process may influence these managers to view the function as a contributing partner and a good investment. It can also help shift the perception that learning and development is a dispensable activity to an indispensable value-adding process. In essence, a comprehensive measurement and evaluation process can transform managers' perceptions from "learning and development is a drain on resources" to "learning and development is a performance partner." These critical shifts in perception come about when managers have convincing evidence that learning and development is not only essential and necessary, but a viable performance contributor to the organization.

Payoff #15: Achieve a Monetary Payoff

Finally, in some situations, an actual monetary payoff can be calculated for investing in measurement and evaluation. This is particularly true with the implementation of the ROI Methodology by which many organizations have actually calculated "the ROI on the ROI." They determine the payoff of investing in the ROI Methodology, which is a comprehensive process generating six types of data. The payoff is developed by detailing specific economies, efficiencies, and direct cost savings generated by the evaluation program.

Many impact studies show how efficiencies can be achieved directly and quickly. Monetary gains are possible when a successful program, as determined by the use of the ROI Methodology, is replicated in other areas, thus, adding value to the organization. Table 3-1 shows a range of ROI studies covering a variety of programs. These programs demonstrate significant returns on investments in learning and development programs.

The monetary payoff is immediate and real when a program not adding value to the organization is eliminated as a consequence of the evaluation. The organization can save much expense by eliminating unnecessary programs.

Table 3-1. Payoff of investing in ROI evaluation as demonstrated in published studies.

Measuring the ROI of . . .	Key Impact Measures	ROI	Reference
Performance Management (Restaurant Chain)	A variety of measures, such as productivity, quality, time, costs, turnover, and absenteeism	298%	Phillips & Phillips (2001)
Process Improvement Team (Apple Computer)	Productivity and labor efficiency	182%	Phillips & Phillips (2001)
Skill-Based Pay (Construction Materials Firm)	Labor costs, turnover, absenteeism	805%	Phillips, Stone & Phillips (2001)
Sexual Harassment Prevention (Health Care Chain)	Complaints, turnover, absenteeism, job satisfaction	1,052%	Phillips, Stone & Phillips (2001)
Safety Incentive Plan (Steel Company)	Accident frequency rate, accident severity rates	379%	Phillips, Stone & Phillips (2001)
Diversity (Nextel Communications)	Retention, employee satisfaction	163%	Phillips & Schmidt (2003)
Retention Improvement (Financial Services)	Turnover, staffing levels, employee satisfaction	258%	Phillips & Phillips (2002a)
Absenteeism Control/Reduction Program (Major City)	Absenteeism, customer satisfaction	882%	Phillips, Stone & Phillips (2001)
Stress Management Program (Electric Utility)	Medical costs, turnover, absenteeism	320%	Phillips, Stone & Phillips (2001)
Executive Leadership Development (Financial)	Team projects, individual projects, retention	62%	Phillips, Stone & Phillips (2001)
E-Learning (Petroleum Industry)	Sales	206%	Phillips, Stone & Phillips (2001)
Internal Graduate Degree Program (Federal Agency)	Retention, individual graduate projects	153%	Phillips & Phillips (2002b)
Executive Coaching (Nortel Networks)	Several measures, including productivity, quality, cost control, and product development time	788%	Phillips & Mitch (2002)

Final Thoughts

Are you now convinced that investment in measurement and evaluation can pay off? Your answer should be an unconditional yes. This chapter outlined the rationale for investing more resources in measurement and evaluation. Although there is some overlap, the 15 specific payoffs represent reasons to increase investment in this critical process. Whatever the motivation, there is immediate value for increasing measurement and evaluation. Some veteran learning and development practitioners have concluded that if there is one item in the budget that deserves more attention, it's measurement and evaluation. This chapter should provide ammunition to justify additional investment in measurement and evaluation. If you are still not convinced, keep reading. Then, try it for yourself.

Part Two

The Building Blocks of Evaluation

Count what is countable, measure what is measurable.
What is not measurable, make measurable.

—Galileo Galilei (1564–1642)

4

Getting Started With Evaluation

• •

The first three chapters detailed the reasons why evaluation fails. They explored the myths that sometimes prevent the implementation of comprehensive measurement and evaluation. The chapters within part two will build a foundation for establishing a measurement and evaluation process within organizations. Today, more executives understand the importance and value of measuring the effectiveness of learning and development programs and are emphasizing this area.

The challenge is to institute a new or enhanced evaluation practice. Achieving success starts with understanding the parameters within which evaluation and measurement must operate. Important first steps are to determine the goals of evaluation and envision how to overcome the barriers. Once these steps are taken, the strategy for organizing, marketing, and implementing the evaluation process becomes clear. Expanding on a current evaluation program can be just as challenging and often involves the same issues.

• •

Where to Begin?

Building an evaluation system involves the three steps shown in figure 4-1. First, setting the stage for evaluation involves looking at the culture, assessing the organization's readiness, and identifying stakeholders and their needs. These issues then lead to the second step: developing the practice by establishing a philosophy, identifying an appropriate model and strategy, and planning the evaluation.

The third step involves implementing the practice, including critical resource allocation for measurement and evaluation. These three steps—setting the stage, developing the practice, and implementing the practice—are covered in this chapter.

Setting the Stage

This initial step in building an evaluation system has four facets: measurement culture, evaluation readiness, the stakeholders, and the stakeholders' needs.

Measurement Culture

If evaluation is relatively new to the organization, you have an excellent opportunity to shape the measurement culture and define what it should be in the future. For most organizations, however, the culture is part of previous experience, history, practices, processes, and procedures. The culture includes the collective perceptions in knowledge of the key stakeholders in the process. They often have a perception or mindset about evaluation and its role in the organization.

If the culture is unsupportive or perhaps dysfunctional, the challenge is to change the culture—often slowly evolving into a desired state. Overcoming this challenge requires application of many of the concepts in this book. As the mindsets, attitudes, and practices are shaped, the measurement culture is defined.

Many organizations speak about having a balanced scorecard. Some organizations go to great lengths to develop comprehensive and detailed functional and operational boundaries. The balanced scorecard provides a four-perspective framework (financial, customer, internal, and learning and growth) to translate strategy into operational terms. Measurement, then, is the language that gives clarity to vague concepts and is used to communicate, not simply to control (Kaplan & Norton, 1992).

Knowing the strategic business goals that fit into this scorecard is necessary for knowing how a learning and development process must be organized. Linking the evaluation process to those strategic goals underscores the importance of speaking the same language as those who manage the business. The evaluation process will not be soft and fuzzy, but tangible and meaningful. The language used to establish and implement evaluation in the organization must be the same language used by the organization's leaders. Carefully examining the organization's scorecard, strategic missions, and goals and determining executive expectations for evaluation are important parts of understanding and establishing a culture for measurement and evaluation.

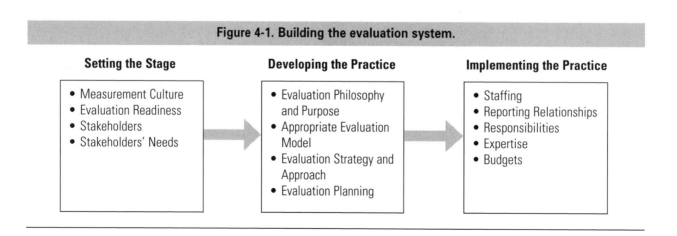

Figure 4-1. Building the evaluation system.

Setting the Stage	Developing the Practice	Implementing the Practice
• Measurement Culture • Evaluation Readiness • Stakeholders • Stakeholders' Needs	• Evaluation Philosophy and Purpose • Appropriate Evaluation Model • Evaluation Strategy and Approach • Evaluation Planning	• Staffing • Reporting Relationships • Responsibilities • Expertise • Budgets

As organizations focus additional efforts on quality, the measurement culture often intensifies. The total quality management and Six Sigma movements brought a variety of new processes and additional measures to enhance the measurement culture. Some organizations pursue recognition of their programs through quality awards such as the Malcolm Baldrige National Quality Award and ISO standards, thus increasing attention to measurement. The bottom line: *The quality movement has stimulated and intensified a measurement culture in organizations.*

Efforts to reinvent, reengineer, transform, and improve organizations have also increased the focus on accountability and measurement. Most reengineering and reinvention initiatives have measurement at the heart of the process; that is, they seek to measure the success of the various processes and solutions. Transformational processes often create measures as part of implementation. Organizational improvement processes often begin with the end in mind with specific measures. Still other processes, such as activity-based costing, cycle time reduction, and customer satisfaction measurement, have focused more attention on the measurement process.

Collectively, these organizational improvement activities define the measurement culture existing today. If these processes are not in place, there is probably a weak measurement culture. With these processes in place, the culture reflects its emphasis, need for, and concerns about measurement and accountability. Often, it is this culture that drives requests for additional measurement and evaluation. For example, when examining the learning and development function, many quality professionals ask, "Can you measure learning and development in the same way that we try to measure other processes?"

Evaluation Readiness

A first step in pursuing a comprehensive measurement and evaluation process is to assess the organization's readiness for such an important effort. Several processes must be in place to ensure that the evaluation process will be supported and sustained.

Exercise 4-1 provides an opportunity to assess your organization's readiness for a comprehensive measurement and evaluation process.

The statements listed in exercise 4-1 are often key indicators of the need for increased measurement and evaluation. Strong agreement with these issues translates into the need for additional measurement and evaluation. When the score is high, there is an urgent need for increased evaluation. You can examine each of the issues in terms of its influence on evaluation, as well as the timing of action for evaluation. For example, if you strongly agree with item 11, it is an important issue that must be addressed now, whereas item 8 is more of a desire and is not time critical. The overall score indicates a degree of urgency as well as the readiness to do something about it.

Stakeholders and Their Needs

Understanding who is a stakeholder in learning and development is important. Technically, everyone in the organization—and maybe some external groups—is a stakeholder in learning and development. Practically, key stakeholders are specific groups with a vested interest in the program. Table 4-1 defines nine major stakeholder groups that exist in large organizations. Small organizations will have some of these stakeholders combined into a small number of groups.

Top Executives. The most important stakeholder group, applicable to all types of organizations, comprises the top executives. These stakeholders—the ones who authorize resources and make commitments to the learning and development process—need to know the scope of learning and development and the volume and efficiencies obtained in the process, which are often labeled indicators (for example, hours, people, costs of learning and development). This information helps executives determine the current investment level in both time and money. More important, they need to see impact and ROI data to be convinced that this investment in learning and development programs is paying off.

Exercise 4-1. Are you ready for measurement and evaluation?

Read each question and check off the most appropriate level of agreement.
A rating of 1 = Disagree
A rating of 5 = Total Agreement

	Disagree				Agree
	1	2	3	4	5
1. My organization is considered a large organization with a wide variety of learning and development programs.	☐	☐	☐	☐	☐
2. We have a large learning and development budget that reflects the interest of senior management.	☐	☐	☐	☐	☐
3. Our organization has a culture of measurement and is focused on establishing a variety of measures including learning and development.	☐	☐	☐	☐	☐
4. My organization is undergoing significant change.	☐	☐	☐	☐	☐
5. There is pressure from senior management to measure results of our learning and development process.	☐	☐	☐	☐	☐
6. My learning and development function currently has a very low investment in measurement and evaluation.	☐	☐	☐	☐	☐
7. My organization has experienced more than one program disaster in the past.	☐	☐	☐	☐	☐
8. My organization has a new learning and development leader.	☐	☐	☐	☐	☐
9. My team would like to be the leaders in learning and development processes.	☐	☐	☐	☐	☐
10. The image of our learning and development function is less than satisfactory.	☐	☐	☐	☐	☐
11. My clients are demanding that our learning and development processes show bottom-line results.	☐	☐	☐	☐	☐
12. My learning and development function competes with other functions within our organization for resources.	☐	☐	☐	☐	☐
13. There is increased focus on linking learning and development programs to the strategic direction of the organization.	☐	☐	☐	☐	☐
14. My learning and development function is a key player in change initiatives currently taking place in my organization.	☐	☐	☐	☐	☐
15. Our overall learning and development budget is growing, and we are required to prove the value of our programs.	☐	☐	☐	☐	☐

Scoring

If you scored:

15–30	You are not yet a candidate for measurement and evaluation.
31–45	You are not a strong candidate for measurement and evaluation, however, it is time to start pursuing some type of process.
46–60	You are a candidate for building skills to implement measurement and evaluation. At this point there is no pressure to show business impact, however, now is the perfect opportunity to improve the evaluation process.
61–75	You should already be implementing a comprehensive measurement and evaluation process, including ROI.

Source: Phillips, P.P. (2002). *The Bottomline on ROI*. Atlanta: CEP Press.

Table 4-1. Key stakeholders and their data needs.

Stakeholders	Data Needs
Top Executives	• Impact and ROI data • Scope and volume (indicators)
Client, Sponsors	• Project approval data • Project results • Impact and ROI data
Middle Managers	• Scope and volume (indicators) • Time commitments • Impact and ROI data
Immediate Managers, Team Leaders	• Time requirements • Roles and duties • Application and impact data
Participants	• Data and time requirements • Feedback on learning • Summary of application and impact data
Learning and Development Leaders, Program Managers, Coordinators	• Summary of reaction, learning, application, impact, and ROI data
Designers/Developers	• Direction, reaction, learning, application, impact, ROI data
Facilitators	• Reaction, learning, application, impact, and ROI data
Evaluator	• All of the above

Clients/Sponsors. The next group of stakeholders is the client or the sponsor of learning and development programs. These individuals initiate, approve, or fund learning and development programs. They need to have data to approve a project as well as data about the results of the project in terms they understand and appreciate. Sometimes this data includes impact and ROI data.

Middle Managers. Middle managers are perhaps one of the most overlooked, yet important, groups. Organizationally, this group of managers fits between the manager of the participant and the top executive group. Collectively, they are larger in numbers than the top executive group, and they,

too, need convincing data about learning and development. In addition to information about the scope and volume of the learning and development function, they need to know about the impact and ROI of specific programs. In their area of operation, they need to understand the value of learning and development to the organization and the time commitments needed to achieve success.

Immediate Managers. The immediate managers of participants (or team leaders) are the direct supervisors of those involved in a learning program. These managers are crucial to the outcome of a learning program; their reinforcement can make a difference in success. They need to understand the time requirements for learning to be effective, and they need to know their specific roles so they can successfully perform their duties. In addition, they need application and impact data so they can be convinced that participants are applying newly acquired skills to the work unit and achieving results.

Participants. Participants are the largest group of stakeholders. These are the individuals (sometimes referred to as consumers, trainees, attendees, learners, or delegates) who are involved in the learning and development program or solution. They need to know what is required from them in terms of data and time. They need feedback on their individual learning and information about application and impact for their group to help them understand the impact of the major learning and development program in which they participate.

Learning and Development Leadership. The learning and development leaders, program managers, and coordinators need a summary of all the information generated in the evaluation process. They need summaries of the reaction, learning, application, impact, and even ROI data, when available and applicable, to help them understand the success and concerns with the learning and development process.

Designers/Developers. Designers and developers need information from the program analyst, usually in the form of objectives at different levels. The objectives drive the design and development process to meet results-based requirements. They also need reaction and learning data from participants to see if adjustments should be made in the learning design. In summary form, they need application, impact, and ROI data, if applicable.

Facilitators. The facilitators, who teach or instruct programs, need reaction and learning data immediately after the program is conducted. This input allows them to make necessary adjustments. Later, they need summary information about application, impact, and ROI data, if available.

Evaluators. Finally, evaluators need all types of data and evaluation information generated about each program. If there is more than one evaluator, they need to share all their information.

There are some universal goals for stakeholder needs, many centered on frameworks such as Kirkpatrick's (1998) and Phillips's (1997) levels of evaluation. All stakeholders usually want to know participants' reactions to learning and development programs. Many believe that all learning should be measured. Others require evidence that learning is being applied in the work environment. Still others discover that they can actually measure the impact of programs on the business, including the monetary benefits compared to the program costs (ROI).

Bell Atlantic Communications managers expected detailed reports of reaction and learning data on a daily basis (Hodges, 1998). They used the data to track the effectiveness of their programs so that they could make changes where changes were needed. They selected particular programs to evaluate for application and business impact.

QUALCOMM, a wireless technology company in San Diego, is very interested in qualitative data. The learning staff invites past participants to luncheons to collect anecdotal data by videotaping the participants' discussions of the program's effectiveness (Hodges, 2002).

Stakeholders and their needs vary with the organization. Before launching a comprehensive evaluation effort, stakeholders must be identified and their needs analyzed. The evaluation system can then be developed to meet those needs. Figure 4-2 shows how the particular needs of stakeholders are linked to the levels of data defined by Kirkpatrick and Phillips. Their needs can often be met by one or more levels of data, which then lead to the evaluation system.

Developing the Practice

Evaluation is defined as a systematic process to determine the value of a program. After the stage has been set, the next step is developing the evaluation process.

Figure 4-2. Evaluation decision tree.

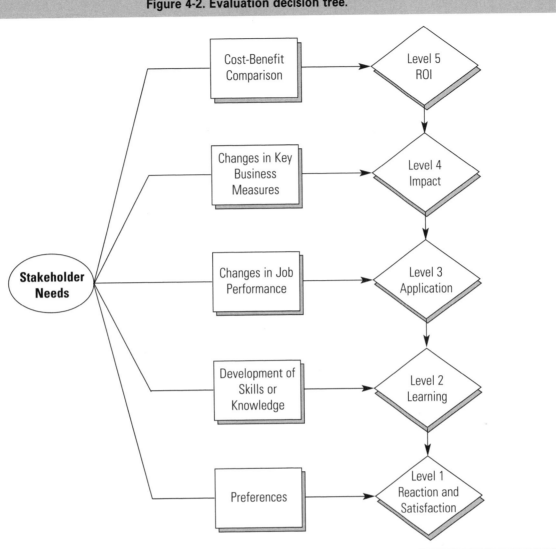

Source: Phillips, P.P., C. Gaudet, and J.J. Phillips. (2003, April). "Evaluation Data: Planning and Use." *Infoline*. Alexandria, VA: ASTD. Reprinted with permission.

Evaluation Philosophy and Purpose

To develop an evaluation process requires that you first establish an overall philosophy and purpose for the evaluation. Begin by researching similar organizations to see if a practice is in place that can be duplicated or can serve as a starting point. Nortel, for example, employed two senior evaluation specialists to help organizational performance managers formulate an evaluation strategy and philosophy. The company's first step was to conduct a benchmarking study of major companies in the telecommunication and computer industries to obtain information on best practices in training evaluation (Falletta & Lamb, 1998).

Evaluation can be undertaken for a broad range of purposes: to improve processes, to decide on the future of a program, or to reinforce results that can be achieved. The following sections briefly describe some common evaluation purposes. Organizations may choose a smaller subset or all of these to develop a philosophy for their evaluations.

Determine Success in Achieving Program Objectives. Learning and development programs should state measurable, specific, and achievable objectives. Evaluation provides input to determine if these objectives have been met. This type of evaluation is appropriate during and after the program.

Identify Strengths and Weaknesses in the Learning and Development Process.

One of the most common purposes of evaluation is to determine the effectiveness of the program and its components. Program evaluation issues may include delivery, learning design, learning environment, program content, learning aids, schedule, activities and exercises, and facilitator. Each component is important to the success of the learning program and must be evaluated to make improvements.

Set Priorities for Learning and Development Resources.

Sometimes evaluation is used to decide which programs should be pursued, which areas are best for program implementation, or both. By collecting relevant evaluation data, you can determine which programs are adding the most value and, therefore, which are the best candidates for additional investment. When budgets are lean and resources are scarce, this purpose of evaluation becomes very important.

Test the Clarity and Validity of Tests, Cases, and Exercises.

Evaluations sometimes provide an opportunity for piloting and validating instruments. Interactive activities, case studies, and tests reflecting the content must be relevant and job related. They must measure the skills and knowledge presented in the program. Measurements of learning provide the necessary information to address these critical issues.

Identify the Participants Who Were Most (or Least) Successful With the Program.

An evaluation can help identify which participants excelled or failed in the learning program. Evaluation may also determine the extent to which participants apply their new skills or knowledge on the job. This information is helpful when determining if an individual should be promoted, transferred, moved up the career ladder, provided additional assignments, or sent back to remedial training. This type of evaluation yields information about the individual as well as the effectiveness of the learning and development program.

Reinforce Major Points Made During the Program.

A follow-up evaluation can reinforce the information covered in a program by attempting to measure the participant's results. The evaluation process reminds participants what they should have applied on the job and the subsequent results that should be realized. In a sense, this follow-up evaluation serves to reinforce to participants the action they should be taking, thus, contributing to the results-based philosophy of many learning and development functions.

Decide Who Should Participate in Future Programs.

Sometimes evaluation provides information to help prospective participants decide if they should be involved in the program. This type of evaluation explores the potential application of the program. It also explores potential enablers and barriers to implementation. Communicating this information to other program participants helps them to decide if participation is desired, needed, or appropriate.

Compare the Benefits to the Costs of a Learning and Development Program.

With increased focus on the bottom line, determining a program's cost effectiveness is critical. This evaluation compares the cost of a program to its value measured in monetary terms. The ROI is the most common measure. Cost-benefit comparison provides management with information needed to eliminate an unproductive program, increase support for programs that yield a high payoff, or to make adjustments in a program to increase the ROI.

Enhance the Accountability of Learning and Development.

In some situations, the accountability

of all expenditures for learning and development has come into question. Evaluation can provide a full array of data to convince top executives, middle managers, and clients that the investment in learning and development is appropriate, that it is being measured and monitored carefully, and that the expenditures are being managed wisely. This ultimate level of accountability is essential in today's competitive environment where resources are scarce.

Assist in Marketing Future Programs. Evaluation can provide marketing data for promoting learning and development programs. In many situations, the learning and development team is interested in knowing why participants attend a specific program, particularly if many programs are offered. Evaluation can provide information to develop a marketing strategy for future programs by determining not only why participants attend the program and who made the decision to attend, but also the success of the program according to specific job groups. Information also can be collected on how participants learned about the program and if they would recommend it to others. All this information provides data for a strategic marketing database.

Determine if a Program Was an Appropriate Solution. Sometimes an evaluation can determine if the program solved the original problem. Too often a learning and development program is conducted to correct problems that, in fact, cannot be solved using training or learning solutions. Other causes—lack of job aids, work flow, systems, procedures, and quality of management—may underlie performance gaps. An evaluation may yield insight into whether learning and development was necessary or, possibly, even provide insight into the correct solution.

Establish a Database to Assist Management With Decision Making. A goal for many evaluation studies is to build a database about the future of learning and development programs. This information can be used by leadership to make decisions about the future of a program or a series of programs. A com-

prehensive system can build a database to help make these decisions. The database can report results in the form of a scorecard that drives many decisions about resources, funding, and priority setting.

Collectively, these purposes define evaluation for a particular organization. The next challenge is to determine the specific model or process to use.

Appropriate Evaluation Model

Determining the appropriate evaluation model, technique, or process can be a challenge. If existing models do not meet the organization's criteria, then it may be necessary to create a new process specifically for the organization. Before making this decision, you should ask several questions:

- Will evaluations be limited to learning and development programs? If not, what other programs will be evaluated?
- Will reaction data be collected? If so, for which programs? What kinds of data are needed?
- Will the data be a part of a database? If so, will an off-the-shelf product be used or a customized one developed?
- How will the data be analyzed and reported?
- Will learning data be collected? If so, how will the data be used?
- Which programs should be evaluated for learning evaluation?
- Does the design team have the necessary skills to develop reliable and valid learning measures?
- Are current learning measures reliable and valid?
- Is there a need to measure job performance? If so, which programs will be measured for job performance change?
- What types of data collection tools will be used?
- Is there a need to measure business value? If so, how will those programs for this level of evaluation be selected?

- What analysis techniques will be employed?
- Will the analysis isolate the performance of the program? If so, what method will be used to isolate?
- Will ROI analyses be needed? If so, which programs will be appropriate for ROI analysis?
- How will the results be reported?

With the number of models currently being offered in learning and development circles, the process of choosing the "best" one can be quite confusing. As presented in chapter 1, one of the disappointments of evaluation is the potpourri of available evaluation approaches and models. Some models include complex formulas, have no basis for soundness, or have never been used regularly by practitioners. To keep the evaluation process from becoming confusing and complex, it is important to adopt a model or a process and use it appropriately and consistently.

Selecting a model used by others helps when making comparisons, benchmarking, and exchanging information. The recommended approach is to develop criteria and then review a small number of feasible models against the criteria (Phillips, 2002). Table 4-2 lists 28 books that present models or practices in measurement and evaluation. The list is not all inclusive, but it does represent models that appear to be most often cited or used within the learning and development profession. No attempt is made here to describe the models or judge them against criteria.

The recommended criteria for an effective evaluation include the following:

1. Evaluation must be *simple,* without complex formulas, lengthy equations, or complicated methodologies. Some models are simple, but many attempts at developing a comprehensive process are in conflict with this requirement. To obtain statistical perfection and precise values, some models have become overly complex and difficult to understand and use. Consequently, they have not been adopted by practitioners.

2. The evaluation model must be *economical* and capable of being implemented without requiring excessive resources. Organizations should be able to make the evaluation model a routine part of learning and development that doesn't require significant additional resources. Sampling and planning are necessary to keep the costs low and make progress with implementation without adding new staff.

3. The assumptions, methodology, and techniques must be *credible.* Logical, methodical steps are needed to earn the respect of practitioners, senior managers, and researchers. A practical approach to evaluation with a user-friendly model is required so that it may be adapted and implemented by practitioners without advanced degrees in research methods, evaluation, or statistics.

4. From a research perspective, the evaluation process must be *theoretically sound and based on generally accepted principles.* Unfortunately, this requirement can lead to an extensive, complicated effort. Ideally, the model selected must strike a balance between a practical and sensible approach *and* a sound and theoretical basis. This is perhaps one of the greatest challenges for those who have offered models for use in evaluation.

5. The evaluation model must *account for other factors that have influenced output variables.* Most models demonstrate the impact of learning and development. When this is accomplished, you need a technique to separate, or isolate, the impact of learning and development from other factors. One of the most overlooked issues—isolating the influence of learning and development—is necessary to build credibility and accuracy with the process and to link learning to business results. Some of the models listed in table 4-2 purposely do not address this issue, leaving the

Table 4-2. Evaluation models and processes listed by year of publication.

Return on Investment in Training and Performance Improvement Programs, 2nd edition. Jack J. Phillips. Butterworth-Heinemann, Woburn, MA. 2003.

The Success Case Method. Robert O. Brinkerhoff. Berrett-Koehler Publishers, San Francisco. 2003.

Linking Learning and Performance: A Practical Guide to Measuring Learning and On-the-Job Application. Toni K. Hodges. Butterworth-Heinemann, Boston. 2002.

Evaluation in Organizations. Darlene Russ-Eft and Hallie Preskill. Perseus Publishing, Cambridge, MA. 2001.

Rapid Evaluation. Susan Barksdale and Teri Lund. ASTD, Alexandria, VA. 2001.

The Targeted Evaluation Process. Wendy L. Combs and Salvatore V. Falleta. ASTD, Alexandria, VA. 2000.

Evaluating Training. Sharon Bartrow and Brenda Gibson. HRD Press, Amherst, MA. 1999.

Measurit: Achieving Profitable Training. Marsha Mondschein. Leathers Publishing, Leawood, KS. 1999.

Results: How to Assess Performance, Learning, and Perceptions in Organizations. Richard A. Swanson and Elwood F. Holton III. Berrett-Koehler Publishers, San Francisco. 1999.

Evaluating Training Programs: The Four Levels, 2nd edition. Donald L. Kirkpatrick. Berrett-Koehler Publishers, San Francisco. 1998.

Evaluating Corporate Training: Models and Issues. Stephen M. Brown and Constance J. Seidner. Kluwer Academic Publishers, Boston. 1998.

Evaluating the Impact of Training. Scott B. Parry. ASTD, Alexandria, VA. 1997.

Handbook of Training and Evaluation and Measurement Methods, 3rd edition. Jack J. Phillips. Butterworth-Heinemann, Woburn, MA. 1997.

Establishing the Value of Training. Sharon G. Fisher and Barbara J. Ruffind. HRD Press, Amherst, MA. 1996.

Evaluating Training Effectiveness, 2nd edition. Peter Bramley. McGraw-Hill, London. 1996.

Evaluating Human Resources, Programs, and Organizations. Byron R. Burnham. Krieger Publishing Company, Malabar, FL. 1995.

Evaluating Training Programs: The Four Levels. Donald L. Kirkpatrick. Berrett-Koehler Publishers, San Francisco. 1993.

Flex: A Flexible Tool for Continuously Improving Your Evaluation of Training Effectiveness. Gary Shouborg. HRD Press, Amherst, MA. 1993.

Make Training Worth Every Penny. Jane Holcomb. Pfeiffer & Company, San Diego. 1992.

The Training Evaluation Process. David J. Basarab, Sr., and Darrell K. Root. Kluwer Academic Publishers, Norwell, MA. 1992.

Training Evaluation Handbook. A.C. Newby. Pfeiffer & Company, San Diego. 1992.

Evaluation: A Tool for Improving HRD Quality. Nancy M. Dixon. University Associates, San Diego. 1990.

Training for Impact. Dana Gaines Robinson and James C. Robinson. Jossey-Bass, San Francisco. 1989.

Achieving Results from Training. Robert O. Brinkerhoff. Jossey-Bass, San Francisco. 1987.

Evaluating Employee Training Programs. Elizabeth M. Hawthorne. Quorum Books, New York. 1987.

How to Measure Training Effectiveness. Leslie Rae. Nichols Publishing Company, New York. 1986.

Evaluation Job-Related Training. Basil S. Deming. ASTD, Alexandria, VA. 1982.

Evaluation of Management Training. Peter Warr, Michael Bird, and Neil Rackham. Gower Press Limited, London. 1970.

Evaluating Training and Development Systems. William R. Tracey. American Management Association, New York. 1968.

results of a study in question. The evaluation model must be able to pinpoint with some degree of accuracy the contribution of the learning program when compared to the other influences.

6. The evaluation model must be *appropriate for a variety of learning and development programs.* Some models apply to only a small number of programs such as sales or productivity training. Others may be used

to evaluate technical training or e-learning. Ideally, the process must be applicable to all types of programs even in soft skills areas such as career development, executive coaching, organization development, change, leadership, and team building.

7. The evaluation process must be *flexible.* You need to be able to apply the evaluation method before the program, during the program, or after the program at specific follow-up times. Today, there are pressures to show the anticipated value from a learning and development program. Although forecasting may be inaccurate, it sometimes is a requirement before expenditures are approved. Consequently, a selected model must have an ROI forecasting component or must be compatible with current forecasting capabilities. Ideally, the process should be able to adjust to a variety of potential timeframes.

8. The evaluation model must be *applicable with all type of data,* including hard data (output, quality, costs, and time) and soft data (job satisfaction, customer satisfaction, other employee- and customer-related areas).

9. The evaluation model must *include a mechanism for developing the costs of the program,* if a cost-benefit analysis is needed. The accountability of learning and development has shifted to the point where clients should know the payoff of programs. The payoff is often expressed as a cost versus benefit. Therefore, the evaluation model must include a way to develop the cost of the solution when needed or requested. Accounting for costs may be particularly important in the forecasting component when the forecast includes the cost versus the benefit.

10. Actual calculations used *must be based on accepted formulas.* This criterion is particularly important for ROI analysis. The concept of ROI is often misused or abused.

An acceptable model must include a formula that is based on generally accepted principles, ideally, those contained in finance and accounting texts. ROI should be defined according to the classical definition: earnings over investment where earnings reflect net benefits, and investment reflects the cost of the program. When benefit-cost ratios are used, they must be based on the same type of calculations where the benefits are divided by the costs. Although other financial terms can be substituted, it is important to use standard financial formulas and terminology in developing the actual amount.

11. The evaluation model must have a *successful track record* in a variety of applications. Although new models are created from time to time, it may be best to stick with a proven method unless a venture with a new model is taken willingly. In far too many situations, models are created but never successfully applied. Although it appears attractive in a magazine article, a model may be impractical, difficult, or impossible to apply in a realistic setting. An effective model should withstand the wear and tear of implementation and achieve the results expected from evaluators and clients.

Other criteria may be added to fit the situation. Figure 4-3 is a tool that can be used to select an evaluation model or process. The process with the highest rating should be the ideal evaluation process unless one or more criteria override. The models listed in table 4-2 provide a beginning point.

Evaluation Strategy and Approach

Determining the overall strategy and approach for evaluation is an important challenge, particularly when pursuing evaluation for major programs. Sometimes you may develop an overall strategy based on general requirements. At other times, you may build a strategy around the evaluation of a

Figure 4-3. Selecting an evaluation model: a criteria checklist.

Compare models against the criteria that are important to your organization.

Rate on a scale of 1 to 5:

A rating of 1 = Does Not Meet Criteria

A rating of 5 = Fully Meets the Criteria

Criteria	Model 1	Model 2	Model 3	Model 4	Model 5	Model 6	Model 7
Credible							
Simple							
Appropriate with a variety of programs							
Economical							
Successful track record							
Theoretically sound							
Accounts for all program costs							
Accounts for all other factors							
Applicable to all types of data							
Applicable on pre-program basis							
Uses appropriate formulas							
Other							
Other							

Source: Phillips, P.P. (2002). *The Bottomline on ROI.* Atlanta: CEP Press. Adapted with permission.

particular program or project. Among the factors that you must consider when developing an evaluation strategy and approach are these:

- location of participants
- duration of the program
- importance of the program in meeting organizational objectives
- relative investment in the program
- reason for the program's existence
- ability of the participants to be involved in evaluation
- level of management interest and involvement in the process
- content and nature of the program
- interest in evaluation by senior management
- availability of business results measures
- feasibility of program enhancements.

These issues relate to key factors that will determine how, when, where, and what will be accomplished in the evaluation of major programs. These issues help frame an overall approach and a strategy for a major project, which translate into specific planning documents described in the next section.

Evaluation Planning

Evaluation planning is critical to the success of an evaluation effort. This topic is described fully in other parts of the book but is briefly explored here. Planning involves three distinct processes:

1. A data collection plan is created to describe how and when the data will be collected. Building from objectives, the planning document defines the measures to be monitored, specific instruments to be used, the sources of data, the timing of data collection, and the responsibilities for data collection.

2. A second planning document—the analysis plan—details how data will be analyzed. This document is essential for programs for which you are conducting an impact analysis. For each business impact measure, this document defines the method used to isolate the effects of the program on each business measure and shows how the data will be converted to monetary values. The analysis plan also details cost categories, any anticipated intangible benefits, and the target audiences for communication of results.

3. Finally, the third plan is the project plan for evaluation. This is a typical project planning tool that defines key steps, milestones, and dates for accomplishing the entire evaluation, beginning with the planning process and ending when all data has been communicated to the various target audiences.

As you might expect, planning is simple for uncomplicated projects and complex for comprehensive projects. For a simple evaluation, only a few items that list the key issues are necessary. All three planning documents may be combined into a single document, comprising less than a page. For a more comprehensive program involving thousands of employees, the evaluation plan may consist of five to 10 pages, detailing specifically how all these issues are addressed. Samples of different evaluation plans can be found in other resources (Phillips & Phillips, 2001; Hodges, 2002).

Implementing the Practice

The final step in the evaluation process addresses staffing, reporting relationships, responsibilities, expertise, and budgets. Each of these components is discussed in the sections that follow.

Staffing

Staffing for evaluation depends on four critical issues in the organization. First, the scope of learning and development determines the extent and complexity of potential evaluation tasks and processes, thus influencing staffing needs. Second, the philosophy of the organization regarding staffing influences the staffing levels. Some organizations prefer to have staff conduct work internally. Others prefer to outsource almost everything leaving only an individual internally to coordinate the work. Third, the resources and budget available influence staffing as well as the access to those individuals who have the time to provide data, collect data, and analyze data. Fourth, the role of evaluation affects staffing. In some organizations, evaluation is a critical part of the process and commands a significant portion of the budget and time. In others, it is a minimal process that commands few resources.

How the evaluation function is organized internally may well depend on who is responsible for the function and the budget allocated to the function. Most organizations designate one person to be responsible for evaluation. This person may be dedicated solely to carrying out evaluations, or this person may have evaluation as just part of his or her job.

There may be no staff, a small staff, or a large staff. With careful planning, an evaluation program can provide meaningful information to the organization. Three situations are presented.

No Evaluation Staff. In this situation, the learning and development staff conduct evaluation along with their many other duties. They may use a variety of external resources, but evaluation is only a part-time function. A variation of this model is appropriate for small organizations where there is a one-person learning and development function. Evaluation responsibilities have to be part time, and the individual responsible may use a variety of low-cost resources to assist with evaluation, but generally this person has to conduct evaluation studies on his or her own. Evaluation projects must be carefully selected because of limited resources. This approach has been used by Apple Computer, among others (Phillips & Phillips, 2001).

Small Evaluation Staff. A second model requires that the individual acquire enough expertise to set up the process for evaluation, develop standards for

the organization, and provide direction for all evaluation studies. This person then directs others in the different lines of business to conduct the evaluations or hire outside consultants to do so. An example of an organization that uses this model is Wachovia Bank where the vice president of assessment, measurement, and evaluation leads a team of about 25 colleagues from different lines of business, each with part-time evaluation and measurement responsibility. Each is certified in the ROI Methodology and operates within an internal ROI network. Regular meetings offer an opportunity to share tools, processes, and experiences. The vice president facilitates these and other evaluation meetings. This model offers the advantage of not having to make a separate financial investment in evaluation for each business unit. However, unless monitored, the evaluation work may become inconsistent, inaccurate, or incomplete.

A variation of this model allows the designated evaluation professional the opportunity to employ a limited staff for evaluation. Bell Atlantic has won awards for innovative performance in evaluation and designated one full-time manager for measurement and evaluation for the entire organization. This manager had a part-time assistant. Because of the size of the organization, the manager established processes for providing reaction and learning data in an automated, standardized manner, requiring little intervention. The manager focused on conducting impact assessments on programs selected according to established criteria. In this model, the manager acquires evaluation expertise and usually outsources the impact studies. The challenge here is that the manager is constantly "training" all the various providers involved in the evaluation efforts because of the need for their involvement due to limited resources. This aspect is particularly challenging when working with a large organization.

Large Evaluation Staff. A third, and sometimes enviable, model is one in which an organization establishes a large staff to conduct evaluations for the organization. Accenture, a large consulting firm, invests in a staff of evaluation professionals, dedicated solely to evaluation. At one time this section had 32 staff members and the focus was on evaluating large training projects. The director of evaluation and performance measurement aligned each team member with different areas or types of programs to build client relationships and to understand the context in which the client needed to operate. The director found that this organizational model provided his company the benefit of allowing the evaluation program to align itself with the strategic mission in multiple areas.

Tennessee Valley Authority (TVA) University, another award-winning evaluation group, has a large evaluation staff. Because of the size and expertise of the staff, the organization is able to go outside the bounds of the typical organizational evaluation program. The evaluation staff design and develop tools and models for evaluation, similar to what a social laboratory would do in an academic environment. They have invested in designing sophisticated models for analyzing reaction, learning, and impact data.

Reporting Relationships

Evaluation can play a major role in ensuring that all performance improvement programs are linked to the organization's overall goals. To do this, the evaluation function must be organized so that the evaluator has the opportunity to communicate with finance, operations, and human resources (HR). Various models are available that may work well within the culture and business framework. Five of the most common are:

- evaluation within HR
- evaluation within the learning and development function
- evaluation within operations
- evaluation within learning design, development, and delivery
- evaluation using external support.

Evaluation Within HR. One approach that is growing in interest is where the evaluation function resides within the HR group. An example of one variation is TD Bank, where all the various divisions of the bank go to HR for evaluation support. The relationship managers represent the different divisions within the bank. They serve as the interface between the divisions and the evaluation staff. This model provides an interface for the different operational areas and can be extremely helpful in meeting evaluation goals because the relationship manager understands the needs, challenges, and metrics of the division or directorate they represent.

This approach has the advantage of not only supporting learning and development, but supporting other HR functions as well. The models and processes used to evaluate employment, employee relations, compensation, benefits, safety and health, and compliance are the same or similar as those used in the evaluation of learning and development.

Evaluation Within the Learning and Development Function. For many organizations, the evaluation staff report directly to the leader of learning and development. The evaluation staff's activities should be combined with the assessment staff's activities so that, collectively, the two processes of assessment (including front-end analysis) and measurement and evaluation are closely integrated. Direct reporting to senior leadership keeps the evaluation and assessment staff independent of the programs.

It is important for the evaluation staff to have regular access to all the individuals involved in learning and development and individuals in other areas such as finance and accounting, operations, and information technology (IT). In some cases, they need to be near the area they support. For example, evaluators in a particular line of business or division or function of the organization may need to be physically located in those areas. It is important for the process to be coordinated and communicated from the perspective of the local managers.

Figure 4-4. Nextel University organization chart.

Nextel is a registered trademark of Nextel Communications, Inc.

An example in which the evaluation function resides within the learning and development function is Nextel Communications University (figure 4-4). Nextel University has separate directorates within the university designated for each line of business. The performance metrics and ROI evaluation group is part of the performance center and reports directly to the vice president of HR development. Each directorate has a representative called a business training manager (BTM) who understands the directorate he or she represents.

This structure works well for Nextel because the vice president of HR development is committed to demonstrating accountability and using evaluation to make their programs strategic. This model offers two main advantages. First, it is important to develop or adopt an evaluation strategy and process carefully so that it is provides credible information and is linked to the organization's strategic vision. The Nextel University organizational structure provides a consistent use of one evaluation model or strategy. Second, the evaluation efforts for each program include the business and operational issues unique to each operational area. However, a tight interface is necessary to ensure that all team members are well informed of the business unit's metrics and needs, goals, and processes of the evaluation function.

Evaluation Within Operations. A third organizational model is one in which the evaluation function resides within each operational line of business. An individual connected with the metrics from that operational line is selected to interface with the learning and development function to determine the impact the programs provide. Here, there is a close alignment between the training function and the business. Boston Scientific, a medical device company, uses this approach. Program needs and evaluation come directly from operations. The evaluators work closely with consumers to ensure learning has an impact. They use evaluation data to make sound tactical and strategic decisions to benefit their line of business. The challenges when using this model, however, are twofold: The organization must ensure these individuals are prepared for their evaluation duties, and the evaluation processes and methodologies used may vary from one line of business to another. Top executives may not be able to see how programs are adding value to the organization overall.

Evaluation Within Learning Design, Development, and Delivery.

A fourth model is where evaluation resides within learning design, development, and delivery. In this case, facilitators are often asked to evaluate their own individual programs. The advantage to this model is that the program designer, developer, or facilitator is intimately familiar with the program to be evaluated, knowing the learning objectives and, in many cases, the application and impact objectives.

Unfortunately, these individuals do not have the skills necessary to conduct effective, comprehensive evaluations. Another challenge to this model is that it is difficult for the individual who is responsible for a program's success to maintain the objectivity required to conduct an effective evaluation of his or her own program. Even if the individuals are able to remain objective, the perceived bias may affect the credibility of the study. Although this is not an ideal model, it is used when the learning and development manager does not appreciate the expertise required to conduct effective evaluations or the professionals themselves are seeking to expand their areas of knowledge and influence.

Evaluation Using External Support.

A final organizational model is one in which the lines of business or HR organization simply uses external support by hiring consultants for individual program evaluations. The advantage to using evaluation consultants is that they are usually quite skilled in conducting effective evaluations. Executives may feel confident in their expertise and experience. Many Japanese organizations, for example, use the JMA Management Center (JMAM) because it has such a good reputation in Japan and is considered to be the best in training evaluation. Toyota Industries Corporation employed JMAM as consultants because Toyota wanted to move beyond reaction-level evaluation for an engi-

neering problem-solving program but did not have the internal capability to go any further (Tsutsumi & Kubota, 2003). An additional advantage to using a consultant is that the organization's staff can benefit from knowledge transfer. The challenge may be that the consultant does not have experience within that particular industry. Also, this can be an expensive approach.

Evaluation Using a Mixed Approach.

Some organizations use a combination of these models, conducting daily evaluations of programs. They may use a consultant to conduct an ROI study on a large, important program. As an alternative, they may hire a consultant to establish the evaluation process and then have their internal staff follow that process. The approach used depends on the organizational culture and degree of evaluation understanding and expertise available. Wherever the evaluation function resides, to be successful it must be situated so that it can work with the HR community including the training designers, developers, and implementers, as well as the stakeholders from the line of business. It also must be structured so that its staff has direct access to finance and accounting so that they can obtain the required approvals and collaboration for a comprehensive evaluation process.

Responsibilities

Regardless of the organizational structure or the allocated staff, the evaluation function must provide credible evaluation services that ensure stakeholder needs are met. The following general responsibilities are for those accountable for implementing a successful evaluation program within their organization:

■ *Establish a standardized model or process for evaluation.* Evaluation results should allow decision makers the opportunity to compare programs, media type, or audience usage. Unless the results have been acquired using a standardized methodology, such comparisons cannot be made.

- *Ensure that the model selected or developed is credible.* Research must be conducted to ensure evaluations can be supported at any stage of data collection, analysis, or reporting.
- *Market the value of evaluation.* An organization may have the most credible method that relies on state-of-the-art tools. But, unless the results are considered of value, the effort and money are wasted. Credible data collection and analysis techniques must be used to gain stakeholder buy-in.
- *Develop the staff.* Recruit, select, train, and foster the professional development of the evaluation staff.
- *Select and manage competent vendor support.* Select evaluation consultants who will support the established framework, strategies, and standards.
- *Research and continually improve data collection and analysis tools.* Ensure that the tools used are efficient and effective and that all evaluations conducted are objective and fair.
- *Manage databases.* Understand the different types of data that will be used for evaluation. Use existing organization databases necessary for analysis. Solicit support from the organization's database managers. Determine where additional databases are needed and build or select them to be both efficient and effective.
- *Budget and manage projects.* Evaluation programs must be completed on time and within budget.
- *Support evaluation activities as needed.* Whether providing support to a new or established evaluation staff or to others in the organization that are conducting evaluations, provide technical and subject matter expertise.
- *Provide performance consulting.* The evaluator today positions evaluation to help ensure transfer and actively seeks ways to link learning to individual performance and individual performance to organizational results.

Specific responsibilities of evaluators depend on their role and their full-time or part-time status. The duties are also both technical and nontechnical. The individuals who are not directly involved in evaluation—designers, facilitators, and program sponsors—also have duties. These duties and responsibilities are presented in more detail in the chapter on implementation.

Expertise

The evaluation staff must have appropriate expertise to accomplish their roles and functions. Traditionally, the skills of evaluation have not always been a part of the preparation for a job in learning and development. However, degree programs in HR development offer evaluation as an integral part of preparation. In addition, a few programs focus on evaluation, measurement, and statistics. Even doctoral degrees are offered in evaluation but rarely in learning evaluation. In most organizations, the expertise must be developed internally or through external resources. Fortunately, many programs and resources are available to build these skills and develop expertise. These are discussed in more detail in the next chapter.

Budgets

The specific budget for evaluation must be determined, and it is usually a function of the learning and evaluation budget combined with the philosophy, scope, and role of evaluation. Budgets are defined in more detail in the next chapter.

Final Thoughts

Getting started in evaluation or increasing emphasis on evaluation is one of the most critical parts of the process. Establishing the framework, philosophy, approach, and culture early can pay dividends in the future.

This chapter explored the major elements of getting starting or taking a fresh look at evaluation. Focusing on such issues as culture, philosophy, readiness, stakeholders, and the various needs of the stakeholder groups, this chapter set the stage for action. It also focused on how to develop and cultivate the evaluation practice. Among the key issues explored were defining the philosophy and purposes, selecting the appropriate evaluation model, developing the strategy and approach, and planning for specific evaluation to be conducted. Finally, the chapter ended with a discussion of some of the key issues involved in implementation such as staffing, reporting relationships, responsibilities, building expertise, and developing budgets. This is an important chapter for individuals currently involved in evaluation or starting an evaluation function from scratch.

5

Resources and Expertise Needed to Make Evaluation Work

• •

This chapter concentrates on building the expertise required for successful evaluation and outlines the budgetary and technological resources required to support evaluation. Although the skills and competencies required for a successful evaluation vary depending on the organization and the philosophy and scope of evaluation, there are many similarities, which are underscored in this chapter. The challenge is to identify the competencies needed for the organization and select a person or people who have those competencies. When such an individual is not available, an alternative would be to develop the necessary competencies following a variety of methods outlined in this chapter. The remainder of the chapter presents information about technology (both hardware and software), the time requirements to implement evaluation, and the budget to make it successful.

• •

Expertise Requirements

The expertise required for implementing measurement and evaluation makes it a rather unique profession. Some professionals have formal preparation in measurement and evaluation, but few are prepared to meet the challenges of today's organizational evaluation needs. Those who have no formal training at all have much to learn. Professionals are needed who can take what has been traditionally an academic discipline and apply it in a real work setting.

As with other comprehensive professions, evaluation involves layers of knowledge. The menu of necessary competencies is constantly changing. Practitioners develop new methodologies, approaches, tools, and standards. A wealth of research, educational programs, and historical information on which to build a foundation is available. Practitioners routinely grow in their profession by using formal and informal ways of developing expertise. Figure 5-1 depicts what many individuals have found to be the progression of their personal growth in evaluation.

The most important issue for the beginner to keep in mind is that there are layers of knowledge in each phase of the progression. Even the expert is learning and growing with each new venture. Regardless of the knowledge or skills acquired, there is always more to learn.

The Beginner

The beginner may have some related formal education such as psychology, education, HR development, organization development, or business. A few may have degrees in evaluation. These professionals have the background for measurement but must learn how to apply it with the most current methods and in nonacademic situations. Those with a behavioral science background may not have a background in education and other types of learning development and must, therefore, learn how to link measurement to learning principles.

Some beginners have a business or financial background with little or no evaluation expertise. Others have no formal education in a field related to learning and development but do have a wealth of job experience. In each of these cases, the evaluator must begin to learn what evaluation competencies successful practitioners possess. This phase takes longer for some than others, depending on their background, willingness to adapt and learn, and ability to acquire new skills quickly.

The beginner must learn the basic principles for evaluation. Perhaps this is why many start with a

Figure 5-1. Progression of evaluation knowledge.

The Expert

The Teacher and Writer

The Diverse Practitioner

The Initial Practitioner

The Beginner

model that provides a path of learning to follow. Models, such as the ROI Methodology, provide specific steps for evaluation with standards and guiding principles (Phillips, 2003). This methodology provides the evaluator a framework on which to build new skills. It can be learned in workshops and is gaining wide appeal throughout the world because professionals from different disciplines can relate to and learn from it. Chapter 4 introduced some other models that are available for practitioners to research and use or adapt to their particular situation. Regardless of the beginner's formal education, some type of foundational training in evaluation should also be provided.

The Initial Practitioner

The initial practitioner has learned basic principles and developed a plan for an evaluation program. Having studied cases and networked with a variety of sources, the initial practitioner is beginning to apply knowledge in evaluation. This phase can be somewhat risky because the initial practitioner invests much time but still has an audience to convince or satisfy. The initial practitioner wants to select a simple case for the first evaluation study—one with specific objectives and easy-to-collect data. This case provides the evaluator the opportunity to practice and, therefore, should not be a highly visible program or one that is likely to yield results that may influence a significant decision. The initial practitioner may need assistance from an expert for the first case.

The Diverse Practitioner

The diverse practitioner has conducted one or more successful evaluation studies and has applied knowledge and expertise to various programs with various objectives. The diverse practitioner has used the evaluation process to compare various media types or different vendors, experimented with different reporting vehicles, and tried new techniques such as ROI forecasting. He or she may have developed, or directed the team to develop, new tools and templates. This is an exciting time for the diverse practitioner—when confidence is building and the contribution to the organization is being recognized. As an evaluation professional, the diverse practitioner is asked to present at internal meetings or external conferences.

The Teacher and Writer

The teacher and writer has much to share. Because so much in the field of evaluation is evolving, publishing successes and challenges is an important way to share information. Preparing for and publishing case studies is an opportunity for the organization and others to see the significant and useful work in which the evaluator has been involved.

After the evaluator has made several successful presentations—both within the organization and externally—he or she may be prepared to teach the topic at workshops and conferences. These workshops include as much theory as is necessary for the participants to understand the principles and techniques for practical application or evaluation. The teacher and writer, therefore, needs solid practical experience.

The Expert

The expert is a recognized leader in the field of measurement and evaluation. He or she has many successful applications and has made a unique contribution to the field. Because of the success with application in today's organization, the expert differs from others who are recognized in measurement and evaluation literature. The expert is also able to quickly adapt his or her expertise to a variety of situations as industry, economy, workplace setting, and organizational trends change. The expert often mentors others.

Knowledge and Skill Requirements

Chapter 4 briefly discussed the roles for the evaluator. To perform those roles, the evaluator needs specific competencies. Various groups have identified the knowledge and skills (or competencies) needed by a successful evaluator. The work of three groups—the Evaluation Consortium, ASTD, and the ROI Institute—is presented here.

The Evaluation Consortium

The first group, the Evaluation Consortium, suggests that the evaluation process performs one or more of the following functions:

- *Positioning:* Evaluation must be positioned correctly within an organization to accomplish its tasks and ensure that it brings meaning and value to the organization.
- *Leading:* Evaluation has the opportunity to both prove value and improve worth. The evaluator should serve as a partner to other organizational areas, demonstrate leadership in meeting organizational goals, and provide innovation in using the best concepts and technology available.
- *Executing:* This is the nuts-and-bolts, roll-up-your-sleeves part of evaluation. Once positioned correctly and leadership is established, the focus is on accelerating and driving performance. The evaluator must take action and conduct evaluations.

Table 5-1 provides the focus for these functions and the associated expertise and abilities required. The table lists expertise and abilities required to be successful in positioning, leading, and executing an evaluation program successfully. Many of the skills and abilities are linked to more than one functional area. Political astuteness and facility, for example, are required to be successful in all three functions. Some of these competencies require formal or informal training, and others reflect attitude or willingness. A manager needs to use these capabilities as a guide when selecting evaluation team members.

ASTD Models

The second source for evaluator competencies is *ASTD Models for Human Performance Improvement*

(Rothwell, 1996). These models suggest that the evaluator "assesses the impact of interventions and follows up on changes made, actions taken, and results achieved in order to provide participants and stakeholders with information about how well interventions are being implemented." In short, the evaluator provides feedback to stakeholders about what benefits were received from a learning and development program or a performance improvement intervention.

The following competencies are linked to the evaluator role:

- *Performance gap evaluation skill:* Measuring or helping others to measure the difference between actual and ideal performance.
- *Ability to evaluate results against organizational goals:* Assessing how well the results of a human performance improvement intervention match intentions.
- *Standard-setting skills:* Measuring desired results of organizations, processes, or individuals; helping others to establish and measure work expectations.
- *Ability to assess impact on culture:* Examining the effects of human performance gaps and human performance improvement interventions on shared beliefs and assumptions about "right" and "wrong" ways of behaving and acting in one organizational setting.
- *Human performance improvement intervention reviewing skills:* Finding ways to evaluate and continuously improve human performance improvement interventions before and during implementation.
- *Feedback skills:* Collecting information about performance and feeding it back clearly, specifically, and on a timely basis to affected individuals or groups (McLagan, 1989).

An update on the competency study was completed in 2004. Table 5-2 shows the key knowledge and actions from the update. The outputs associated with the competencies are listed in table 5-3.

Table 5-1. Evaluation function, focus, and expertise and abilities.

Function	Focus	Expertise and Abilities
To Position	• Determine key receivers and decision makers • Market the value of evaluation • Communicate performance gaps and opportunities	• Research skills • Structural analysis skills • Writing skills • PowerPoint design skills • Facilitation skills • Presentation skills • Needs analysis skills • Political facility • Positive power and influence (marketing) skills • Listening skills • Coaching capabilities • Patience for different agendas
To Lead	• Articulate vision • Identify leading indicators • Use modeling to predict performance • Communicate to get buy-in on recommendations for performance improvement	• Strategic planning skills • Performance analysis skills • Business acumen, both relationship and consulting • Ability to make complex data simple, intuitive, and actionable • Ability to find data sources • Ability to research design methods • Predictive and descriptive statistics skills • Communication skills • Modeling skills • Political facility • Ability to collaborate with and coach colleagues
To Execute	• Select or develop an evaluation framework • Design and implement a measurement strategy • Recruit, select, train, and foster the professional development of evaluation staff • Select and manage competent vendor support • Create and continually improve data collection and analysis tools • Manage databases • Collect, manage, and analyze data • Use statistics to describe • Plan, budget, and manage projects • Support evaluation activities • Provide performance consulting	• Ability to understand data types • Test construction and validation • Data analysis, housing, and reporting skills • Ability to know the limits and benefits of evaluation methods and tools • Guideline and standard development skills • Ability to connect with benchmarking data and professional development opportunities • Consulting skills • Organizational understanding • Survey design skills • Understanding of data gathering technologies • Ability to think independently and creatively • Tenacity • Ability to identify root causes and primary needs in a given situation • Project management skills • Performance consulting skills • Relationship management skills • Ability to analyze data in relation to research questions • Implementation planning skills • Operations management skills • Ability and willingness to mentor • Instructional design knowledge • Political astuteness

Source: Based on the Business Alignment Framework developed by the Evaluation Consortium, a group of evaluation professionals from various organizations throughout the United States.

Table 5-2. Key knowledge and actions.

Measuring and Evaluating:	
Gathering data to answer specific questions regarding the value or impact of learning and performance solutions; focusing on the impact of individual programs and creating overall measures of system effectiveness; leveraging findings to increase effectiveness and provide recommendations for change.	
Key Knowledge	• Statistical theory and methods • Research design • Analysis methods, such as cost-benefit analysis, ROI, etc. • Interpretation and reporting of data • Theories and types of evaluation, such as the four levels of evaluation
Key Actions	• *Identifies customer expectations:* Works with customers or stakeholders to determine why they are interested in measurement and what they hope to accomplish with the results; clearly defines research questions, expectations, resources available, and desired outcomes of the measurement project; manages unrealistic expectations.
	• *Selects or designs appropriate strategies, research design, and measures:* Uses customer questions and expectations to guide the selection or design of appropriate strategies, research designs, and quantitative and qualitative measurement tools; employs a variety of measures and methods to reduce bias and ensure objective conclusions; identifies appropriate samples sizes, data tracking methods, and reporting formats; balances practical implications of rigor, effort, real-life constraints, and objectivity to create a workable approach.
	• *Communicates and gains support for the measurement and evaluation plan:* Summarizes measurement approach into a clear plan that can be communicated to customers and stakeholders; communicates timelines, roles/responsibilities, and identifies other project management needs; gains buy-in for the plan and ensures that all parties understand the approach and their responsibilities.
	• *Manages data collection:* Ensures that all data collection methods are applied consistently and objectively; monitors ongoing data collection to ensure that assumptions required for statistical inference are being met; manages and documents data in a format that can be adequately manipulated during the analysis process (e.g., spreadsheets).
	• *Analyzes and interprets data:* Creates descriptive and inferential summaries of data in a format that can be readily understood and communicated; adheres to rules of statistical analysis to reduce bias and provide adequate support for conclusions; uses a process of creative inquiry to fully explore the data and all of its possible implications and meaning.
	• *Reports conclusions and makes recommendations based on findings:* Provides data summaries in a format that can be readily understood and interpreted by customers and stakeholders (potentially multiple summaries); organizes information in a way that directly responds to research questions; bases recommendations and conclusions on sound analysis methods; clarifies customer questions and the meaning of the data.

Source: Bernthal, P.R., K. Colteryahn, P. Davis, J. Naughton, W.J. Rothwell, and R. Wellins. (2004). *ASTD 2004 Competency Study: Mapping the Future*. Alexandria, VA. ASTD. Used by permission. www.astd.org.

Table 5-3. Outputs associated with the evaluator role.

Evaluator Role	Terminal Output
Assesses the impact of interventions and follows up on changes made, actions taken, and result achieved in order to provide participants and stakeholders with information about how well interventions are being implemented.	Written and oral reports to: • Participants and stakeholders about the progress of an intervention • The organization about performance • The organization about progress of interventions • Work groups or teams about their performance • Work groups or teams about the progress of interventions • Management about performance • Management about interventions
Evaluator Competencies	**Enabling Outputs**
1. Performance Gap Evaluation Skills: Measuring or helping others to measure the difference between actual performance and ideal performance.	• Human performance improvement evaluation objectives • Human performance improvement evaluation designs and plans • Human performance improvement evaluation instruments • Pre- and post-program measures of worker performance • Evaluation findings, conclusions, and recommendations • Reports to management and workers on the outcomes of human performance improvement strategies
2. Ability to Evaluate Results Against Organizational Goals: Assessing how well the results of a human performance improvement intervention match intentions.	• Linkage of human performance improvement interventions to other change efforts of the organization • Linkage of each human performance improvement intervention with other interventions • Linkage of human performance improvement interventions to organizational plans, goals, and objectives • Linkage of human performance improvement interventions to organizational/business needs
3. Standard Setting Skills: Measuring desired results of organizations, processes, or individuals; helping others to establish and measure work expectations.	• Work standard/expectations established • Work standard/expectations communicated
4. Ability to Assess Impact on Culture: Examining the effects of human performance gaps and human performance improvement interventions and shared beliefs and assumptions about "right" and "wrong" ways of behaving and acting in one organizational setting.	• Linkage of human performance improvement interventions to organizational culture performance improvement
5. Human Performance Improvement Intervention Reviewing Skills: Finding ways to evaluate and continuously improve human performance improvement interventions before and during implementation.	• Written and oral reports to stakeholders and participants about the progress of an intervention.

(continued on page 60)

Table 5-3. Outputs associated with the evaluator role (continued).

Evaluator Competencies (continued)	Enabling Outputs (continued)
6. Feedback Skills: Collecting information about performance and feeding it back clearly, specifically, and on a timely basis to affected individuals or groups (McLagan, 1989).	• Feedback to the organization about performance • Feedback to the organization about progress of interventions • Feedback to work groups or teams about performance • Feedback to work groups or teams about progress of intervention • Feedback to management about performance • Feedback to management about interventions

Source: Rothwell, W. (1996). *ASTD Models for Human Performance Improvement: Roles, Competencies, and Outputs.* Alexandria, VA: ASTD. Used by permission. www.astd.org.

Taken together, the role, competencies, and work outputs of the evaluator dramatize the importance of the role for collecting, feeding back, and emphasizing the benefits received from performance improvement interventions.

Evaluators must demonstrate results in measurable improvements in performance. They may also be asked before a learning program is undertaken to forecast what results are expected from it so that a sound investment decision can be made as to whether to expend the time and resources to implement the program in the first place (Rothwell, Hohne & King, 2000). Figure 5-2 shows how measurement and evaluation is integrated into the general model for workplace learning and performance. Measurement and evaluation is one of the most important focus competencies, necessary for success.

The ROI Institute

The third source for evaluator competencies is the ROI Institute (www.roiinstitute.net). It develops skills for individuals involved in the implementation of the ROI Methodology. In preparation for this assignment, individuals usually obtain special training to build specific skills and knowledge in the ROI process. The role of the implementation leader is broad and includes a variety of specialized duties. The leader can take on many roles, as shown in table 5-4.

At times, the ROI implementation leader serves as technical expert, giving advice and making deci-

sions about some of the issues involved in evaluation design, data analysis, and presentation. As an initiator, the leader identifies programs for ROI analysis and takes the lead in conducting a variety of ROI studies. When needed, the implementation leader is a cheerleader, bringing attention to the ROI Methodology, encouraging others to become involved, and showing how value can be added to the organization. Finally, the implementation leader is a communicator, letting others know about the process and communicating results to a variety of target audiences. All the roles come into play at one time or another as the leader implements ROI in an organization.

The specific skills needed by the ROI implementation leader are defined in table 5-5. These skill sets reflect the progression of knowledge of an evaluator, described earlier, by offering initial essential skills and developing expertise with higher-level skills sets. These skills differ from those suggested by the Evaluation Consortium or the ASTD competency studies. These skill sets focus on higher-level evaluations required in many organizations today by showing value added.

The first seven skill sets relate to the model used in the ROI Methodology, which generates six types of data. A skill set is offered for each major part of the model (J.J. Phillips, 2003). Two of these skills—isolating the effects of learning and converting data to monetary value—are critical and challenging in today's comprehensive measurement and evaluation systems.

Figure 5-2. Workplace learning and performance competency model.

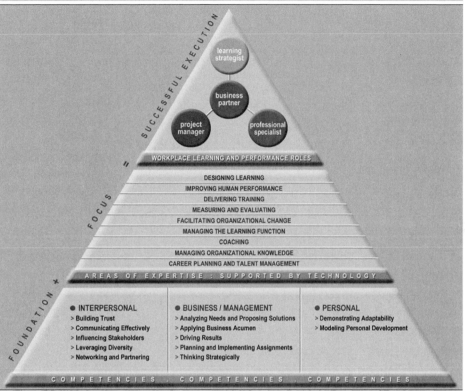

Source: Bernthal, P.R., K. Colteryahn, P. Davis, J. Naughton, W.J. Rothwell, and R. Wellings. (2004). *ASTD 2004 Competency Study: Mapping the Future.* Alexandria, VA. ASTD. Used by permission. www.astd.org..

Isolating the effects of learning is an absolute when a learning and development program is evaluated at the business impact level. This skill uses 10 different techniques to isolate the effects of a learning program from other influences, thus connecting the impact of learning to business results.

Without this skill, it is difficult to connect learning to business.

The second critical skill is converting data to monetary value. This skill is a necessity when there is a desire to know the value a learning and development program has contributed to the organization.

Table 5-4. Potential roles of the implementation leader.

Technical expert	Cheerleader
Consultant	Communicator
Problem solver	Process monitor
Initiator	Planner
Designer	Analyst
Developer	Interpreter
Coordinator	Teacher

Table 5-5. Skill sets for ROI implementation leaders.

1. Planning for ROI calculations
2. Collecting evaluation data
3. Isolating the effects of training
4. Converting data to monetary values
5. Monitoring program costs
6. Analyzing data including calculating the ROI
7. Presenting evaluation data
8. Implementing the ROI Methodology
9. Proving internal consulting on ROI
10. Teaching others the ROI Methodology

Today, values are often expressed in monetary terms. If an ROI calculation is desired, it is necessary to convert the business impact data to monetary value to compare with the cost to develop the ROI.

Another important skill set is the implementation process in which much of the focus is on making evaluation successful, routine, and sustainable, within the desired budget. The skills have at least 10 subcomponents to make evaluation routine in the organization. The last two skill sets build the capability necessary to become an expert, focusing on consulting within the organization and teaching others the evaluation process. These capstone skill sets develop the capability to reach the expert level in the progression of knowledge for the evaluator.

Building Evaluation Expertise

Various sources are available to help practitioners acquire the expertise needed to be a successful evaluation practitioner. These sources range from formal education to networking.

Formal Education

Evaluators have a variety of academic programs available to them, including educational psychology/organizational psychology, educational measurement and research, evaluation, HR development, and business administration.

As evaluation has evolved into a field of linking learning and business performance, many institutions with various academic programs have added measurement and evaluation courses to the curriculum. Some institutions offer an evaluation degree, usually at the master's or doctoral level. For most evaluation academic degrees, the setting is in government or educational sectors such as health care, policy, educational program, and a variety of social programs initiated for or by the public sector. This type of academic background may not be suitable for measuring learning and development in a private sector business.

Professional Organizations

Several professional organizations offer memberships for evaluators or those interested in evaluation. ASTD (www.astd.org) offers a special membership option—the ASTD ROI Network. In 2004, the ASTD network had 600 members. Through this network, a variety of methods and vehicles are available to exchange information and develop member expertise and capabilities. The vision statement for the ASTD ROI Network is: "To be the recognized global leader in the science and practice of ROI measurement and evaluation." The mission statement is: "The ASTD ROI Network promotes individual and organizational improvement and accountability through education, research, publication, and practice. We advance the sharing of measurement and evaluation best practices and expertise in order to demonstrate the ultimate financial contribution of performance and organizational improvement."

The American Evaluation Association (www.eval.org) is primarily for those involved in evaluation education, government health care, and nonprofit organizations. Although membership is across all segments, most of the members are in the education and public sector.

The ROI Institute is available for those who have completed certification on the ROI Methodology (www.roiinstitute.net). The ROI Institute is a research, information, and benchmarking organization designed to provide workshops, research, and advice in the area of measurement and evaluation, including the ROI Methodology. The individuals who complete certification in the ROI Methodology become members of the institute. Others may visit the Website to obtain additional information. The ROI Institute conducts a variety of educational programs, including workshops and certification. In 2004, there were approximately 2,000 members of the Institute.

The Evaluation Consortium is a group of evaluation professionals from various organizations throughout the United States. Memberships are usually in the range of 10–15 organizations who meet to exchange information. There is no Website or email contact for the Consortium. For additional information on this group, contact the authors.

The membership of the International Society for Performance Improvement (www.ispi.org) comprises individuals improving human performance in the workplace. Members work for all kinds of businesses, including industry, government, education, and military. Although there is no particular evaluation membership option for ISPI, several products and services focus on evaluation topics. ISPI's human performance improvement standards include measurement and evaluation.

The Society for Human Resource Management (www.shrm.org) provides a variety of services for individuals involved in the HR management field. Although there is no membership option for those with a special interest in evaluation, many of their programs and conferences address evaluation topics.

Books and workshops are offered through SHRM and focus on the evaluation process as well.

Collectively, these professional organizations provide an opportunity for individuals to learn, grow, develop, and build expertise in measurement and evaluation. More important, they provide the opportunity for networking with others in similar roles.

Conference Providers

A variety of conferences that focus directly on measurement and evaluation are available. ASTD, through the ROI Network, offers three conferences dedicated exclusively to measurement, evaluation, and ROI. One such meeting occurs during the annual ASTD International Conference and Exposition as a "conference within a conference." In addition, the ASTD ROI Network offers a stand-alone conference in a city within the United States and a city outside the United States. These conferences are equally spaced during the calendar year and provide participants an opportunity to hear from practitioners, discuss case studies, and exchange information on measurement and evaluation.

Several specialty conferences on measurement and evaluation are often provided. HR Events, a division of the International Quality and Productivity Center (www.sharedservicesnetwork.com), routinely offers measurement and evaluation for both the learning and development and HR fields. For example, in February 2004, HR Events offered its Eighth Annual HR Measurement Week in Las Vegas, billed as the industry leading conference in HR measurement, strategies, methods, and outcomes. At the same time, a two-day conference on Measuring and Benchmarking Training Projects and Programs was offered in the same city. Other conference providers in Europe, Asia, and South America offer education opportunities for the evaluation professional.

The annual conference sponsored by *Training* magazine is another opportunity for measurement and evaluation. The Training and Online Learning Conference and Expo (www.vnulearning.com) offered each year is an excellent opportunity to learn more about measurement and evaluation. As part of the annual conference, a measurement and ROI certificate program is offered where individuals can obtain certification sponsored by the ROI Institute.

Some conferences target specific industries. For example, the ASTD ROI Network (www.astd.org) offers a special conference each year on ROI in government that focuses on the use of the ROI Methodology in the public sector at the federal level. In addition, the University of Southern Mississippi (www.usm.edu/wlpc), through its Work-place Learning and Performance Center, presents an annual conference, ROI in the Public Sector. This conference focuses on measurement, evaluation, and ROI in the government sectors at the state, local, and federal levels and discusses a variety of evaluation issues including implementation.

The annual conference of the American Evaluation Association (www.eval.org) represents an excellent opportunity to learn about methodology and new applications for the evaluation field. Most of the attendees are involved in the public, educational, and health sectors.

Finally, the annual conference of the Society for Human Resource Management (www.shrm.org) and the International Society for Performance Improvement (www.ispi.org) offer workshops and conference topics on measurement and evaluation.

All these conferences offer rich opportunities for learning new applications, exploring new techniques, reaffirming existing processes, and networking with a variety of individuals in the same field.

Workshops

Workshops represent an opportunity to learn specific measurement and evaluation skills. Although many workshop opportunities are available, three specific organizations focus on long-term, sustained workshops for measurement and evaluation professionals. ASTD ROI Network offers a standard two-day workshop on ROI. This competency-building workshop focuses on collecting data, isolating the effects of the program, converting data to monetary costs, calculating ROI, and presenting data to target audiences.

ASTD offers a one-day overview of ROI—The Bottomline on ROI—which shows the benefits, barriers, and basics of measurement, evaluation, and ROI. Finally, ASTD offers a three-day measurement and evaluation workshop that focuses on evaluating reaction, learning, and application. A five-day certification program is offered by the ROI Institute (www.roiinstitute.net). This intense workshop teaches participants how to implement a comprehensive measurement for any evaluation process, including ROI.

The Evaluators Institute (www.eval.org) offers a variety of programs in January and July through specially designed workshops covering such issues as data analysis, data collection, and evaluation methodology.

In addition to these providers, the conferences described previously often have pre- or postconference workshops on measurement and evaluation connected with them.

Certification

The only sustained certification available to build skills in measurement and evaluation is the certification for the ROI Methodology. This comprehensive program is designed for individuals who are assuming a leadership role in the implementation of measurement and evaluation including ROI. The process involves prework and preparation prior to attending a one-week workshop. The comprehensive workshop is designed to build the 10 skills essential for ROI implementation leaders (see table 5-5).

During the workshop, the participants plan a project for ROI evaluation, develop data collection and ROI analysis plans for the project, and present it to the team for feedback. In addition, participants develop and present a plan to show how they will help implement the ROI Methodology in their organization, addressing issues under their control. The typical participant is charged with the responsibility of implementing ROI, or a part of it, in his or her division or organization. Sometimes, participants are part of a team and the entire team attends.

A public version was offered in 1995 when it became apparent that many organizations wanted to send one or two individuals to this type of session to develop the skills to lead the implementation of ROI. They did not, however, have the resources to send the entire team to an internal certification workshop. More than 2,000 individuals have attended a certification workshop, representing some 1,000 organizations in 35 countries. Almost a third of this group had an internal team certified. Others sent one or two individuals to a public workshop. The adoption has been widespread, with certification conducted on several continents. Certification is unique, and no other process is available to satisfy these critical needs. It still enjoys internal and public success.

On-the-Job Learning

In addition to industry-provided education, many opportunities are available to learn evaluation on the job using knowledge sharing, team training, expert briefings, impact study reviews, and other formal and informal on-the-job learning methods. Because most learning occurs on the job, developing a structured on-the-job learning program enhances the acquisition of skills and leads to measurement standards that are consistent throughout the organization. Inviting experts to assist with projects has the added benefit of developing new skills. Active learning can be beneficial to evaluators as they learn and apply evaluation processes. As each impact study is completed, the project team should debrief others who need to know more about techniques, processes, barriers, and enablers.

TD Bank of Toronto adopted the policy of "research and apply, research and apply" for establishing and testing a new evaluation process. This approach not only ensured that the process was based on sound theory but also kept the staff active and focused as they tested the theory in application.

Tapping Into a Network

Because measurement and evaluation is new to many, it is helpful to have a group of peers who are likely experiencing similar issues and frustrations. Tapping into an international network (already developed), joining or creating a local network, or building an internal network are all possible ways to use the resources, ideas, and support of others.

In 1996, the ROI Network was created to exchange information among the graduates of the ROI certification workshop. During certification, the participants bond and freely exchange information with each other. The ROI Network is an attempt to provide a permanent vehicle for information exchange and support, accessing all groups involved in certification.

The ROI Network, a professional organization which claims about 600 members, is now affiliated with ASTD and is poised for growth. The network operates through a variety of committees and communicates with members through newsletters, Websites, email distribution lists, and annual meetings. The ASTD ROI Network represents an opportunity to build a community of practice for measurement, evaluation, and ROI.

In some situations, it may be appropriate to develop a group of local individuals who have the same interest in and concerns about measurement. When this is the case, a local network may be feasible. For some occasions, the local network may involve the entire country (such as the Dutch ROI Network); in other cases, the network may operate in a more confined area (such as the Puerto Rico ROI Network). In Puerto Rico, a group of 30 individuals, who participated in the certification process, challenge each other to remain as an intact group to discuss issues and report progress. Members come from a wide variety of backgrounds but meet routinely to present progress; discuss problems, barriers, and issues; and plan next steps. This is a very active group, typical of what can develop if individuals are willing to share information and support each other.

Another way to integrate the needs of evaluation practitioners is through an internal network. The experience with networks—in organizations where the idea has been tried—shows that these communities of practice are powerful tools for both accelerating evaluation skill development and cultivating a new culture of accountability. For example, Wachovia Bank, a large financial services organization in the United States, has an internal network of 25 evaluation professionals who meet at least quarterly to discuss strategies, barriers, and opportunities.

The concept of a network is simplicity itself. The idea is to bring people who are interested in measurement and evaluation together throughout the organization to work under the guidance of trained evaluators. Typically, advocates within the learning and development department see both the need for beginning networks and the potential of evaluation to change how the department does its work. Interested network members learn by designing and executing real evaluation plans. This process generates commitment for accountability as a new way of doing business for the department.

Technology Requirements

Much technology is available to support evaluation execution and reporting needs. The evaluator needs to research and select from the many vendors and programs available, pinpointing the most appropriate technology for the organization. Hardware and software can support almost any phase of the evaluation, including data collection, data management and reporting, and data analysis.

Data Collection

Because reaction data is collected for most learning and development programs, you can exploit technology to collect, store, and report data. Some organizations want to collect learning and application data regularly from surveys, adding to the need to collect and distribute data.

For small organizations, the technology available in most office suite applications enables the evaluator to organize, tabulate, and store data. For medium-sized organizations, data input can be made more efficient with scanning tools. A variety of scanning hardware and software packages are available, such as Scantron, which allows data to be input, stored, combined, and reported automatically. Many organizations are moving to systems for online input whereby participants in learning and development programs provide feedback information at reaction, learning, and application levels. Data is collected, organized, and presented routinely in a variety of different reports. KnowledgeAdvisors (knowledgeadvisors.com) offers a software package called Metrics that Matter to aid data collection and reporting.

Much technological help is available for designing, administering, and analyzing surveys and questionnaires. For example, SurveyPro, SurveySays, SurveyTracker, and QuestionMark are just a few of the software packages available to help design and administer this most common data collection tool.

Data Management and Reporting

For larger organizations, software is needed to help organize and manage learning and development system data. These learning management systems, which essentially manage the complete learning process, often have an evaluation component. Systems are available from SumTotal Systems, Saba, and other suppliers.

Sometimes these systems provide evaluation data in a summary report usually referred to as a training or learning scorecard, which is a summary of all the data collected and organized around the levels of evaluation. Figure 5-3 shows one type of scorecard that presents a variety of data of different programs (Schmidt, 2003). The data is arranged by levels, and several measures such as monetary values, application measures, business impact measures, and ROI values, if available, are also included. The software available from KnowledgeAdvisors (Metrics that Matter) has the capability to build scorecards from data across programs.

Figure 5-3. Example of a scorecard for evaluation data.

Learning and Development Scorecard

Level of Evaluation	Participant Reaction				Learning	Application	Business Impact	ROI
	Registration/ Logistics	Design	Delivery	Impact				
Programs								
Program 1								
Program 2								
Program 3								
Program 4								
Program 5								
Program 6								

Data Analysis

The data analysis required for the evaluation of most learning and performance improvement programs does not require sophisticated statistical analysis, so a robust system may not be necessary. Microsoft Excel, which is included in Microsoft Office Suite, is usually sufficient. This software summarizes and describes the data in terms of the mean, range, standard deviation, and so forth. It can perform the analysis required to conduct trend line analysis, hypothesis testing, and correlation analysis. Excel can create bar graphs, pie charts, and other acceptable methods for displaying data. Other statistical packages, such as SPSS, SAS, STAT-PACK, DataDesk, Statview, and MINITAB can conduct additional analyses. The important thing is to keep the analysis simple.

Software programs designed specifically for comprehensive evaluation are now available. Programs start at the beginning point of evaluation and move through the various stages of data collection, analysis, processing, and reporting. In some cases an impact study is generated. Programs available from KnowledgeAdvisors are comprehensive and designed specifically for high-level evaluation, usually involving impact and ROI analysis.

Time Requirements

The time requirements for collecting, analyzing, and reporting evaluation data depend on the level of evaluation addressed, the resources available, the expertise of the staff, and the technology used. Using standardized processes for collecting reaction, learning, and application data reduces the time needed for each evaluation. Of course, outsourcing evaluation studies can also reduce the time requirements, as well as increase the level of automation used for various tasks related to evaluation data.

With so many potential variations, it is impossible to pinpoint the length of time it takes to conduct an evaluation study. Nevertheless, a rough estimate can provide some insight into time requirements. Table 5-6 offers estimates based on the authors' combined experience. It is important to remember that these estimates vary with the type of study, setting, and methods utilized. As the table reveals, automation drastically reduces the amount of time required

Table 5-6. Approximate time needed for evaluation.

Level of Evaluation	Approximate Time Requirement (in hours)	
	Manual	Automated
Reaction and Satisfaction (Level 1)	1–2	<1
Learning Assessments and Simple Tests (Level 2)	2–6	<1
Application and Behavior Changes (Level 3)	18–24	3–5
Impact Analysis (Level 4)	36–54	4–8
Return-on-Investment (Level 5)	48–80	12–18

Notes:
Includes data collection, analysis, and reporting
Excludes time necessary for planning, design, data integration across programs, and meetings to present data
Assumes that higher-level evaluation includes data at lower levels

to conduct evaluation studies at all levels. Because the variances are smaller, more reliable predications can be developed when automation is used.

Table 5-6 also assumes that higher-level evaluations include data collected at lower levels. For example, when an impact analysis (level 4) is conducted, data is also collected at levels 1, 2, and 3. It is assumed, for these estimates, that such data is available for input for the higher-level evaluation, providing evidence of the chain of impact and clearly showing the target audience how the participants reacted, learned, applied, and secured results with the program.

Initial planning for a major study should take no more than a day. The time to design the instruments can vary depending on the number of instruments and method of data collection. Data collection is the most variable part of the analysis. Simple data collection instruments, such as questionnaires, are inexpensive and involve less time to implement. Other instruments, such as observation, interview, and focus groups, are more time consuming and can add considerably to the time estimates to this table. Nevertheless, table 5-6 is a rough guide of the time required to conduct evaluation studies. The greatest variance occurs with impact and ROI studies for which the setting, type of program, type of data collected, and the variety of instruments used can significantly influence the time required.

This table reveals several important principles about the time for evaluation:

- The processes should be automated to the extent possible. Fortunately, there are software packages available to help make data collection routine and consistent.
- The design time can be very significant and should be automated if possible.
- The use of standardized tools and templates is extremely helpful.
- The programs destined for impact and ROI analysis should be limited to those considered to be significant, critical, expensive, highly visible, and time consuming. This selection

process helps manage the resource requirements and keeps the commitments low for the overall time required for evaluation.

It takes a considerable amount of time to establish the evaluation system so it becomes routine, automated, and replicable. It may take six months to a year to build a system necessary for a comprehensive measurement and evaluation process for a large organization. For example, figure 5-4 presents a timeline for building a system for a major *Fortune* 500 organization. This organization used the evaluation data to develop scorecards. External consultancy support and automation were critical parts of the process. Such is the case for many large organizations that have large budgets and need to conduct evaluation over several hundred programs.

Cost and Budget Requirements

Budgeting for evaluation depends on all the issues presented in chapter 4 (purpose, philosophy, strategy, staffing, and so forth). Table 5-7 lists the items that should be included in the budget.

Table 5-7 shows the typical cost categories of any process involved in learning, development, and performance improvement. Evaluation should be considered a major component of the performance improvement cycle and should be included in the budgeting process just as design, development, implementation, and initial analysis are. The most significant cost is the value of staff time allocated for evaluation.

Participant costs reflect the cost of the participants' time required for evaluation activities. For example, if a participant is involved in a focus group, he or she is not able to take customer orders or work on the assembly line. This item is handled in different ways. In some situations, participant time is not a budgeted item and is considered negotiable. But, when the time involved in evaluation is significant and requires time away from work to provide input and data for evaluation issues, the costs are included.

Figure 5-4. Timeline for establishing an evaluation system.

Evaluation Activity	1	2	3	4	5	6	7	8	9	10	11	12
Design and Pilot Reaction Survey	▓	▓										
Construct and Validate Learning Measures		▓	▓									
Research Vendor Database Support			▓	▓								
Customize Vendor Tool				▓								
Design Internal Database				▓	▓	▓	▓					
Integrate with Internal System				▓	▓	▓						
Select Studies for Impact Analysis					▓							
Conduct Impact Studies					▓	▓			▓	(average time per study)		
Design Reporting Format									▓			
Plan for and Communicate Results										▓	▓	▓

Month

Table 5-7. Budgeting for evaluation.

Evaluation Item	Cost
Salaries & Employee Benefits for L&D Staff (No. of staff × avg. salary × employee benefits factor × no. of hours on evaluation project)	
Meals, Travel, and Incidental Expenses	
Participant Costs (for time involved in evaluation)	
Fees and Licenses	
Office Supplies and Expense of Printing Materials	
Outside Services	
Technology	
General Overhead Allocation	
Other Miscellaneous Expenses	
Total Evaluation Costs	

The line item for outside services includes consultants' fees and external services for evaluation. Fees and licenses include fees for staff to attend programs or other learning activities to build expertise with evaluation and may also include license agreements to use certain technologies or processes for evaluation. Technology includes both hardware and software used to support the evaluation process. This item may be prorated if the hardware or software is used for other functions in the organization.

Organizations with some history of using evaluation likely have data from prior evaluations to determine costs for evaluation budgeting. Those new to evaluation or who are improving the evaluation process significantly may need help with evaluation costs. Table 5-8 shows a sample of cost items associated with evaluation. Some of these are based on actual cost, some are estimates based on benchmarking data from evaluation implementations, and others are some guesses.

The total cost of measurement and evaluation as a percentage of the budget, taken from benchmarking, is probably the most valuable item. For comprehensive evaluations, for which data is collected on every program and a few programs are taken to the levels of impact and ROI, the cost can be as much as 3 to 5 percent of the total learning and development (or performance improvement) budget. The budget figure should include all the direct items in a typical budget including staff salaries, office expense, and external charges.

The cost of processing one evaluation questionnaire varies, but many external providers charge about $2 or less per questionnaire for processing and reporting back to the organization. At this price, a program with 25 participants can be summarized and reported to appropriate groups for $50.

The cost of conducting impact studies varies significantly as already shown. The costs shown in table 5-8 are based on the authors' experience. The cost of an impact or ROI study is typically 5 to 10 percent of the total cost of the project. For example, in a major learning and development program that costs an organization $200,000, the evaluation cost should be in the range of $10,000–$20,000. These are only rough guides and can vary considerably.

Table 5-8. Typical costs of selected evaluation items.

Evaluation Item	Approximate Cost
Total cost of measurement and evaluation as a percentage of learning and development budget—best practice	3%–5%
External cost of processing one reaction questionnaire	$2.00
Application/behavior change study (internal)	$2,000–$3,000
Application/behavior change study (external)	$15,000–$20,000
Impact/ROI study (internal)	$5,000–$10,000
Impact/ROI study (external)	$15,000–$50,000
Cost of an impact/ROI study as a percentage of project costs	5%–10%
Fee to attend ASTD two-day workshop on measurement, evaluation, and ROI	$850[†]
Fee to attend ASTD one-day workshop on bottomline on ROI	$450[†]
Cost of SurveyPRO (for questionnaire design and administration)	$1,500
Fee for certification in the ROI Methodology	$2,995
Cost to join the ASTD ROI Network	$75[†]
Cost to attend ASTD ROI Network Conference	$795[†]
Cost of *Handbook of Training Evaluation and Measurement Methods,* 3rd edition (Phillips, 1997)	$62.50
Cost of multicolor, fold-out process model for the ROI Methodology*	0
Value of an effective, efficient, state-of-the-art evaluation system	Priceless

* Available from the lead author, at no charge.
† Prices reflect ASTD membership.

The other cost items are offered just to show a sampling of different costs and to provide a bit of humor in what may be considered a boring issue.

Final Thoughts

Planning for evaluation takes into account many factors, including expertise and resources. Expertise can be acquired from several sources such as formal education, professional workshops, organizations, conferences, on-the-job training, and external resources. Data collection and analysis must be carefully planned to consider technology and time requirements. A variety of technology options are available to assist in data collection, analysis, and reporting. Using technology drastically reduces the amount of time required for these activities. Budgetary requirements depend upon the decisions made regarding evaluation purpose, role, and strategy. Planning for evaluation costs should be a routine part of the budgeting process.

Regardless of resources available, every organization should be able to establish and implement an evaluation program that provides appropriate data about the success of learning, development, and performance improvement programs.

6

Communicating and Using Evaluation Results

Now that you have evaluation data in hand, what's next? Should the data be used to modify the program, change the process, show the contribution, justify new programs, gain additional support, or build goodwill? How should the data be presented? Who should present the data? Where should the data be communicated? These and other questions are examined in this chapter.

The worst course of action is to do nothing. Communicating results is as important as achieving them. Using many examples, this chapter provides useful information to help present evaluation data to the various audiences using both oral and written reporting methods. Next, the strategies for using evaluation are explored. Evaluation data should drive improvement because most studies provide data to change or adjust processes to enhance results.

Principles of Communicating Results

The skills required to communicate results effectively are almost as delicate and sophisticated as those needed to obtain results. Style is as important as substance. Regardless of the message, audience, or medium, a few general principles apply. Because they are important to the overall success of the communication effort, these general principles should serve as a checklist for the learning and development staff when disseminating program results.

Communication Must Be Timely

Usually, you should communicate results as soon as they are known. From a practical standpoint, it may be best to delay the communication until a convenient time, such as the next management meeting, quarterly sales meeting, or annual IT conference. Questions of timing must be addressed. Is the audience ready for the results considering other things that may have happened? Is the audience expecting results? When is the best time for having the maximum effect on the audience? Are there circumstances that dictate a change in the timing of the communication?

Target Communications to Specific Audiences

Communication is more effective if it is designed for a particular group. The message should be specifically tailored to the interests, needs, and expectations of the target audience. The results described in this chapter reflect outcomes at all levels of evaluation. Some data is developed earlier in the project and communicated during the project. Other data is collected after implementation and communicated in a follow-up study. Therefore, the results, in their broadest sense, may range from early feedback with qualitative data to ROI values in varying quantitative terms.

Select Communication Media Carefully

For particular groups, some media may be more effective than others. Face-to-face meetings may be better than special bulletins. A memo distributed exclusively to top management may be more effective than the company newsletter. Choosing the most appropriate method of communication can help improve the effectiveness of the process.

Communication Should Be Unbiased and Modest

Facts must be separated from fiction and accurate statements from opinions. Various audiences may accept communication from the learning and development staff with skepticism, anticipating biased opinions. Boastful statements sometimes turn off recipients, and most—if not all—of the content is lost. Observable, credible facts carry far more weight than extreme or sensational claims. Although such hyperbole may get audience attention, it often detracts from the importance of the results.

Communication Must Be Consistent

The timing and content of the communication should be consistent with past practices. A special communication at an unusual time during the program may provoke suspicion. Also, if a particular group, such as top management, regularly receives communication on outcomes, it should continue receiving communication—even if the results are not positive. If some results are omitted, you might leave the impression that only positive results are reported.

Audience Perception Influences Communication Strategy

The reputation of the learning and development staff is an important consideration when developing the overall strategy. Opinions are difficult to change, and a negative opinion of the learning and development staff may not change with the mere presentation of facts. However, the presentation of facts alone may strengthen the opinions held by those who already agree with the results. Facts help reinforce their position and provide a defense in discussions with others. A staff with a high level of credibility and respect may have a relatively easy time communicating results. Low credibility can create problems when trying to be persuasive.

Planning the Communication Is Critical

You must carefully plan your communications to produce the maximum results. Planning is important to ensure that each audience receives the proper information at the right time and that appropriate actions are taken. Several areas need some attention as the policies are developed, specifically:

- What will actually be communicated?
- When will the data be communicated?
- How will the information be communicated?
- Where will the communication take place?
- Who will communicate the information?
- Who are the target audiences?
- What specific actions are required or desired?

These general principles are important to the overall success of the communication effort. They should serve as a checklist for the learning and development staff when disseminating program results.

Selecting Audiences for Communications

To the greatest extent possible, the learning and development staff should know and understand the target audience. The staff should find out what information is needed and why. Each group has its own needs relative to the information desired. Some want detailed information; others want brief information.

Input from others may be needed to determine audience needs. The staff should try to understand audience bias as each audience has a particular bias or opinion. Some will quickly support the results, whereas others may be against them or be neutral. The staff should be empathetic and try to understand differing views. With this understanding, communications can be tailored to each group. This is especially critical when the potential exists for the audience to react negatively to the results.

When approaching a particular audience, the following questions should be asked about each potential group:

- Are they interested in the evaluation study?
- Has someone made a commitment regarding communication?
- Is the timing right for this audience?
- Is this audience familiar with the program?
- How do they prefer to have results communicated?
- Do they know the team members?
- Are they likely to find the results threatening?
- Which medium will be most convincing to this group?

The potential target audiences for evaluation results are varied in terms of job levels and responsibilities. Determining which groups receive a particular communication deserves careful thought, as problems can arise when a particular group receives inappropriate information or when another is omitted altogether. A sound basis for proper audience selection is to analyze the reason for communication, as discussed in an earlier section. Table 6-1 shows common target audiences and the basis for selecting each audience.

Perhaps the most important audience is the sponsor—the individual or team supporting the evaluation study. The sponsor initiates the program, reviews data, and weighs the final assessment of the effectiveness of the program. Another important target audience is the top management group, which is responsible for allocating resources to the program and needs information to help justify expenditures and gauge the effectiveness of the efforts.

Selected groups of managers (or all managers) are also important target audiences. Management's support and involvement in the process and the department's credibility are important to success. Effectively communicating program results to management can increase both support and credibility.

Communicating with the participants' team leaders (or immediate managers) is essential. In many cases, team leaders must encourage participants to implement the program. Also, they often

Table 6-1. Rationales for communicating to specific target audiences.

Primary Target Audience	Reason for Communication
Sponsor, Top Executives	To secure approval for the program
Managers, Team Leaders	To gain support for the program
Participants, Team Leaders	To secure agreement with the issues
Top Executives, Managers	To build credibility for learning and development
Immediate Managers	To enhance reinforcement of the processes
Sponsor, Learning and Development Staff	To drive action for improvement
Team Leaders, Participants	To prepare participants for the program
Participants	To enhance results and quality of future feedback
Sponsor, Learning and Development Staff	To show the complete results of the program
Sponsor, Learning and Development Staff	To underscore the importance of measuring results
Sponsor, Learning and Development Staff	To explain techniques used to measure results
Team Leaders, Participants	To create desire for a participant to be involved
Top Executives, Managers	To stimulate interest in learning and development
All Employees	To demonstrate accountability for expenditures
Prospective Sponsors, Managers, Team Leaders	To market future programs

support and reinforce the objectives of the program. Positive results enhance the commitment to learning and improve the credibility of the learning and development staff.

Occasionally, results are communicated to encourage participation in the program, especially for programs offered on a voluntary basis. The potential participants are important targets for communicating results.

Participants need feedback on the overall success of the effort. Some individuals may not have been as successful as others in achieving the desired results. Communicating the results adds additional pressure to effectively implement the program and improve results for the future. For those achieving excellent results, the communication serves as reinforcement of what is expected. Communicating results to participants is often overlooked, with the assumption that because the program is complete, participants do not need to be informed of its success.

The learning and development staff must receive information about program results. For small projects, the learning and development staff should receive an update; for large projects, the complete team should be involved. Those who design, develop, facilitate, and implement the program must be given information on the program's effectiveness, so that adjustments can be made if the program is not as effective as it could be. The support staff should receive detailed information about the process to measure results. This group provides support services to the learning and development team.

All employees and stockholders may be less likely targets. General interest news stories may increase employee respect for learning and development. Goodwill and positive attitudes toward the organization may also be by-products of communicating results. Stockholders, on the other hand, are more interested in the return on their investment.

Although table 6-1 shows the most common target audiences, there may be others in a particular organization. For example, management or employees could be divided into different departments, divisions, or even subsidiaries of the organization. The number of audiences can be large in a complex organization. At a minimum, four target audiences are always recommended: a senior management group, the participants' immediate manager or team leader, the participants, and the learning and development staff.

Developing the Impact Study

The type of formal evaluation report depends on the extent of detailed information needed for the various target audiences. Brief summaries of results with appropriate charts may be sufficient for some communication efforts. In other situations, particularly with significant programs requiring extensive funding, a detailed evaluation report may be necessary. This report contains in-depth information for specific audiences and various media.

The report may consist of the following sections:

- *Executive summary:* This brief overview of the entire report explains the basis for the evaluation and the significant conclusions and recommendations. It is designed for individuals who are too busy to read a detailed report. It is usually written last but appears first in the report for easy access.

- *Background information:* This section provides a general description of the learning and development program. If applicable, the needs assessment that led to the implementation of the program is summarized, including the events that led to the evaluation. Other specific items necessary to provide a full description of the program are included.

- *Objectives:* The goals for both the impact study and the learning and development program are outlined. The report details the particular objectives of the study itself so that the reader clearly understands the rationale for the study and how the data will be used. In addition, specific objectives of the learning program are detailed, as these are the objectives from which the different types or levels of data will be collected.

- *Evaluation strategy:* This section outlines all the components that comprise the total evaluation process. The specific purposes of evaluation are outlined, and the evaluation design and methodology are explained. Any unusual issues in the evaluation design are discussed. Finally, this section provides any other useful information related to the design, timing, and execution of the evaluation.

- *Data collection and analysis:* The evaluator explains in this section the methods used to collect data. The instruments used in data collection are described and presented as exhibits. The methods used to analyze data are presented, including methods to isolate the effects of the program and convert data to monetary values.

- *Program costs:* Itemized costs are listed in this section, which includes a summary of the costs by category. For example, analysis, development, implementation, and evaluation costs are recommended categories for cost presentation. The assumptions made in developing and classifying costs are briefly discussed in this section of the report.

- *Reaction and satisfaction results:* The evaluator details the data collected from key stakeholders (the participants involved in the process) to measure reactions to the program and levels of satisfaction with various issues and parts of the process. Other input from the sponsor or managers may be included to show the levels of satisfaction.

- *Learning results:* This section briefly summarizes the formal and informal methods for measuring learning. It explains how participants have learned new processes, skills, tasks, procedures, and practices.

- *Application and implementation results:* Here, the evaluator shows how the program was actually implemented and the success with the application of new skills and knowledge. Implementation issues are addressed, including any major successes (or lack thereof).

- *Business impact results:* This section (if applicable) shows the actual business impact measures reflecting the business needs that provided the basis for the program. This data summary shows the extent to which business performance has changed because of the program implementation.

- *ROI results:* This section (if applicable) shows the ROI calculation along with the benefit-cost ratio. It compares the ROI value to the value that was expected and provides an interpretation of the ROI calculation.

- *Intangible benefits:* The evaluator demonstrates in this section how various intangible measures were directly linked to the program. Intangibles are those measures purposely not converted to monetary values.

- *Barriers and enablers:* This section discusses the various problems and obstacles inhibiting the success of the learning program, presented as barriers to implementation. Also, factors or influences that had a positive effect on the program are included as enablers. Together, they provide insight into what can hinder or enhance programs in the future.

- *Conclusions and recommendations:* Here, the evaluator offers conclusions based on all the results. If appropriate, brief explanations are presented on how each conclusion was reached. A list of recommendations or changes in the program, if appropriate, is provided along with brief explanations for each recommendation.

These components make up the major parts of a complete evaluation report. Figure 6-1 shows the table of contents from a typical evaluation report for an evaluation. This report is an effective, professional way to present data. The methodology should be clearly explained, along with assumptions made in the analysis. The reader should readily see how the results were developed and how the specific steps were followed to make the study conservative, credible, and accurate. Detailed statistical analyses should be placed in the appendix.

Because this document reports the success of the group of employees, complete credit for the success must go to the participants and their leaders because their performance generated the success. Boasting about results should be avoided. Although the evaluation may be accurate and credible, it still may have some subjective issues. Huge claims of success can quickly turn off an audience and interfere with the delivery of the desired message.

Selecting Communication Media

Many options are available to communicate program results. In addition to the complete impact

Figure 6-1. Example outline for an evaluation report.

I. Executive Summary
II. General Information
    A. Background
    B. Objectives of Study
III. Methodology for Impact Study
    A. Levels of Evaluation
    B. Collecting Data
    C. Isolating the Effects of Training
    D. Converting Data to Monetary Values
    E. Assumptions

> Builds credibility for the process

IV. Data Analysis Issues
V. Program Costs
VI. Results: General Information
    A. Response Profile
    B. Success With Objectives
VII. Results: Reaction and Satisfaction (Level 1)
    A. Data Sources
    B. Data Summary
    C. Key Issues
VIII. Results: Learning (Level 2)
    A. Data Sources
    B. Data Summary
    C. Key Issues
IX. Results: Application and Implementation (Level 3)
    A. Data Sources
    B. Data Summary
    C. Key Issues
X. Results: Business Impact (Level 4, optional)
    A. General Comments
    B. Linkage With Business Measures
    C. Key Issues
XI. Results: ROI and Its Meaning (Level 5, optional)
XII. Results: Intangible Measures
XIII. Barriers and Enablers

> The results with six measures:
> Levels 1, 2, 3, 4, 5, and Intangibles

    A. Barriers
    B. Enablers
XIV. Conclusions and Recommendations
    A. Conclusions
    B. Recommendations
XV. Exhibits

study document, the most frequently used media are meetings, interim and progress reports, the organization's communication tools, email, brochures, Websites, and case studies.

Meetings

In addition to meetings with the sponsor to discuss results, other meetings are fertile opportunities for you to communicate program results. All organizations hold a variety of meetings where learning and development results can be an important part of the agenda. For example, routine staff meetings, designed to review progress, discuss current problems, and distribute information, may be an appropriate venue to discuss results of a program in that area. Management meetings, leadership meetings, best practices meetings, and business update meetings are all possibilities to discuss results of major programs. A summary of results can be integrated into these meetings to build interest, commitment, and support. You can highlight results along with operating issues, plans, and forecasts.

Interim and Progress Reports

Although usually limited to large evaluation projects, a highly visible way to communicate results is through interim and routine memos and reports. Published or disseminated via the intranet on a periodic basis, these reports are designed to inform management about the status of the program, to communicate the interim results achieved in the program, and to activate needed changes and improvements. A more subtle reason for the report is to gain additional support and commitment from the management group. This report is produced by the learning and development staff and distributed to a select group of stakeholders in the organization. Although the format and scope may vary considerably, common topics include schedule of activities, reactions from participants, results, and participant spotlight. When produced in a professional manner, the report can improve management support and commitment to the evaluation effort.

The Organization's Communication Tools

To reach a wide audience, the learning and development staff can use in-house publications. Whether a newsletter, magazine, newspaper, or Website, these types of media usually reach all employees. The information can be quite effective if communicated appropriately. The scope should be limited to general interest articles, announcements, and interviews.

Email and Electronic Media

Internal and external Webpages on the Internet, company-wide intranets, and email are excellent vehicles for releasing results, discussing progress, and informing employees and other target groups about learning and development results. Email, in particular, provides a virtually instantaneous means to communicate results to large groups.

Brochures and Pamphlets

A brochure might be appropriate for programs conducted on a continuing basis, for which participation is voluntary. A brochure should be attractive and present a complete description of the program, with a major section devoted to the results achieved. Measurable results and reactions from participants or even direct quotes from individuals could add spice to an otherwise dull brochure. Also, the results may provide convincing data that the program is successful.

Case Studies

Case studies represent an effective way to communicate the results of a learning and development program. Some major evaluation projects should be developed in a case study format. A typical case study describes the situation, provides appropriate background information (including the events that led to the implementation of the program), presents the techniques and strategies used in the study, and highlights the key results in the program.

Case studies tell an interesting story of how the evaluation was developed and the problems and concerns identified along the way. Case studies provide a way to document history about the program and its success to convince prospective sponsors that learning and development programs add value, and to communicate to external groups about the success with learning and development.

Communicating the Information

Perhaps the greatest challenge of communication is the actual delivery of the message. You can deliver the message in a variety of ways and settings, based on the target audience and the media selected for the message.

Three particular approaches deserve additional coverage. The first approach is feedback throughout a major project to ensure that information flows so changes can be made. The second approach is presenting an impact study to a senior management team—one of the most challenging tasks for an evaluator. The third approach is communicating regularly and routinely with the executive management group.

Each approach is explored in more detail in the sections that follow.

Providing Feedback During Program Implementation

One of the most important reasons for collecting reaction, learning, and application data is to provide feedback quickly so adjustments or changes can be made in the program. In most programs, data is routinely collected and quickly communicated to a variety of groups. Some feedback sessions result in identifying specific actions needed to make changes. This process becomes comprehensive and should be managed in a very proactive way.

Block (2000) offers some tips for providing feedback and managing the feedback process:

- Communicate quickly—within days or a week or two—to let individuals involved in the program have the information as soon as possible.
- Keep the data simple by condensing it into an understandable, concise presentation.
- Examine the role of the learning and development staff and the program's sponsor in the feedback situation by anticipating potential reactions to the data and the actions that need to be taken.
- Use negative data in a constructive way by pointing out that it is now known which areas need to change.
- Present positive data in a cautious way—almost in a discounting mode.
- Use descriptive, focused, short, and simple language for the meeting and communications.
- Ask the sponsor for reactions to the data.
- Ask the sponsor for recommendations about what might be needed to keep a project on track or put it back on track if it derails.
- Act on the data by weighing the different alternatives to discern the changes that will be necessary.
- Secure agreement from all key stakeholders to make sure everyone is on board with the adjustments and changes deemed necessary.
- Keep the feedback process short; avoid protracted meetings or lengthy documents. If this occurs, stakeholders will avoid the process instead of being willing to participate in the future.

Following these steps can help move the project forward and provide important feedback, often ensuring that adjustments are supported and made.

Presenting Data to Senior Management

One of the most challenging and stressful communications is presenting the evaluation report to the senior management team, a group that usually serves as the sponsor of a program or evaluation study. The challenge is to convince this highly skeptical and critical group that outstanding results have been achieved, if indeed they have.

Communication of results must occur within a reasonable timeframe, address salient points, and ensure the managers understand the process. Two particular issues can create challenges. First, if the results are very impressive, it may be difficult to garner buy-in from the managers—to get them to believe the data. On the other extreme, if the data is negative, it can be a challenge to keep managers from overreacting to the negative results and starting to look around for someone to blame. Several guidelines can help make sure this process is planned and executed properly:

- Plan a face-to-face meeting with senior team members after the first one or two major impact studies. If the executives are unfamiliar with the evaluation methodology, a face-to-face meeting is necessary to ensure they understand the process. Executives will probably attend the meeting because they may not have previously received impact data about the success of learning and development programs. It will usually take an hour for this presentation.
- When making the initial presentation, distribution of the results should be postponed until the end of the session. The early focus

of the meeting should be on the evaluation methodology, process, and assumptions. It is important for the audience to understand the methodology before data and conclusions are presented.

■ Explain the evaluation process, step by step. This part of the presentation shows how and when the data was collected, who provided the data, and how the data was isolated from other influences and converted to monetary values. The various assumptions, adjustments, and conservative approaches are presented along with the total cost of the program, if applicable.

■ When you present results, reveal the data items one level at a time. Starting with reaction data (level 1), the presentation moves through the levels, and ends with the intangibles. This sequence allows the audience to see the chain of impact of reaction to learning, to application, to business impact, and to ROI, if applicable. After some discussion on the meaning of the ROI, the intangible data is presented. The time to present each level may vary depending on audience needs. Usually, the lower levels require less time. This approach helps overcome the potentially negative reactions to a very positive or negative ROI, if the ROI is developed.

■ Show the consequences of additional accuracy, if it is an issue. The tradeoff for more accuracy and validity is increased expense. Address this issue whenever necessary, agreeing to add data if needed.

■ After a group has had a face-to-face meeting with a couple of presentations, communications may be streamlined. After executives understand the evaluation process, a shortened version, such as an executive summary, may suffice. As the audience becomes more familiar with the process, an even shorter version of the evaluation report may be appropriate, which

will involve a one- to two-page summary with charts or graphs showing all six types of measures. Figure 6-2 shows a sample of a one-page summary.

■ Make adjustments for next communications. Collect concerns, reactions, and issues for the process and make adjustments accordingly for the next presentation or type of communication.

Collectively, these steps will help you prepare for and present one of the most critical meetings with the management team (Phillips, 2000).

Communication With Executive Management and Sponsors

No group is more important than the top executives when it comes to routine communication of results. In many situations, this group is also the sponsor. Improving communications with this group requires developing an overall strategy, which may include some or all of the following actions:

■ *Strengthen the relationship with executives:* An informal, productive relationship should be established between the learning and development manager and the top executive at the location where the program is implemented. Each should feel comfortable discussing needs and results. One approach is to establish frequent, informal meetings with the executive to review problems with current projects and discuss other performance problems and opportunities in the organization. Frank discussions can provide the executive with insight not possible from any other source.

■ *Show how learning and development programs have helped solve major problems.* Although hard results from recent programs are comforting to an executive, solutions to immediate problems may be more convincing. This issue represents an excellent opportu-

Figure 6-2. Example of a one-page summary of the impact study.

Impact Study

Program Title: Preventing Sexual Harassment

Target Audience: First and Second Level Mgrs (655); Secondary: All employees through group meetings (6,844)

Duration: 1 day, 17 sessions

Techniques to Isolate Effects of Program: Trend analysis; participant estimation

Techniques to Convert Data to Monetary Value: Historical costs; internal experts

Fully Loaded Program Costs: $277,987

Results

Level 1: Reaction	Level 2: Learning	Level 3: Application	Level 4: Impact	Level 5: ROI	Intangible Benefits
93% provided action items	65% increase posttest vs. pretest Skill practice demonstration	96% conducted meetings and completed meeting record 4.1 out of 5 on behavior change survey 68% report all action items complete 92% report some action items complete	Turnover reduction: $2,840,632 Complaint reduction: $360,276 Total improvement: $3,200,908	1,051%	Job satisfaction Reduced absenteeism Stress reduction Better recruiting

Source: Phillips, P.P., and H. Burkett. (2001, November). Managing Evaluation Shortcuts. *Infoline*, No. 250111. Alexandria, VA: ASTD. Reprinted with permission.

nity to discuss future programs for impact analysis or ROI evaluation.

- *Distribute program results routinely.* When a program has achieved significant results, make appropriate top executives aware of them. This can easily be done with a one-page summary (see Figure 6-2) outlining what the program was supposed to accomplish, when it was implemented, who was involved, and the results achieved. Routine information on major evaluation projects, as

long as it is not boastful, can reinforce credibility and accomplishments.

- *Ask executives to be involved in a review of learning and development.* An effective way to build commitment from top executives is to ask them to serve on a learning and development review committee. This committee provides input and advice to the learning and development staff on a variety of issues, including needs, problems with the present programs, and evaluation issues.

Analyzing Reactions to Communication

Ultimately, the best indicator of how effectively evaluation data has been communicated is the level of commitment and support from the management group. The allocation of requested resources and a strong commitment from top management are tangible evidence of management's perception of the results of programs. In addition to this top-level reaction, there are a few techniques the learning and development staff can use to measure the effectiveness of their communication efforts.

Whenever results are communicated, the reaction of the target audiences can be monitored. These reactions may include nonverbal gestures, oral remarks, written comments, or indirect actions that reveal how the communication was received. Usually, when results are presented in a meeting, the presenter has some indication of how the results were received by the group. During the presentation, questions may be asked or, in some cases, the information may be challenged. Tabulating these challenges and questions can be useful way to decide on the type of information to include in future communications. Positive comments about the results are desired and, when they are made—formally or informally—they should also be noted and tabulated.

Learning and development staff meetings are an excellent arena for discussing the reaction to communicating results. Comments may come from many sources depending on the particular target audiences. Input from different members of the staff can be summarized to help judge overall effectiveness.

When major program results are communicated, a feedback questionnaire may be used for an audience or a sample of the audience to determine the extent to which the audience understood or believed the information presented. Questionnaires are practical only when the effectiveness of the communication has a significant impact on future actions.

The purpose of analyzing reactions is to make adjustments in the communication process if necessary. Although the reactions may involve intuitive assessments, a more sophisticated analysis can provide more accurate information to make these adjustments. The net result should be a more effective communication process.

Using Evaluation Data

Evaluation is a process improvement tool that should drive changes to improve unacceptable results or provide recommendations to enhance current success. In addition, evaluation data can provide useful information to enhance the image, credibility, and success of learning and development and provide recognition to all the stakeholders involved. This chapter explores the strategies for using evaluation data properly and capturing improvements generated from the evaluation data.

Adjust Program Design

Perhaps one of the most important reasons for evaluation is to make changes in the design of the program. This strategy is particularly appropriate in the early stages of the launch of a new learning and development solution. Reaction and learning data can be used to spot problems with content, learning design, and sequencing. This information can be quickly provided to designers and developers to make adjustments as needed. Even follow-up application and impact data may reveal design flaws or situations where design features need to be adjusted to enhance success.

Improve Program Delivery

Delivery is a key issue to providing learning and development, and input about the quality of the delivery is usually obtained directly from participants. The typical facilitator evaluation is a major component of reaction and satisfaction evaluation. Participants provide an assessment on the preparation, quality, knowledge, and capability of the facilitator. This information can be quickly provided to facilitators (sometimes at the end of the session) so that adjustments can be made.

In addition to the facilitator feedback, additional information about delivery may be collected including information on the channel of delivery (instructor-led, self-study, on-the-job, or e-learning). Because delivery is critical to the acceptance and effectiveness of learning, information can be obtained to make important adjustments. Reaction, satisfaction, and learning data may be critical at this stage. Some organizations use statistical process control concepts to measure responses for reaction data. Upper and lower limits are established beyond which action is needed. For example, when a program is routinely offered and ratings are consistently high, there may be no reason to take action. But if ratings drop significantly or are much higher, additional inquiry, investigation, and possible action are needed.

Influence Application and Impact

Sometimes a measurement is taken to reinforce to participants what they should be accomplishing. In effect, the measurement is actually reminding them of what they should be doing and the success they should be achieving.

This use of data is particularly appropriate with follow-up questionnaires provided in advance of the time the questionnaires are due. Participants are made aware of expectations that influence the success of the program. Some evaluators argue that this use of data is unfairly biasing the evaluation; measurements influence success. If, however, the designers are convinced that this measurement is adding value, then it may be helpful to include it every time so that success can be enhanced. It then becomes a permanent part of the process.

Enhance Reinforcement for Learning and Development

One of the most difficult challenges is to entice managers of participants to provide reinforcement for learning and development. Evaluation data can show these managers the success (or lack of success) of their reinforcement efforts. Sometimes the data

can make a convincing case for managers to provide additional reinforcement or to be recognized and rewarded for their successful reinforcement efforts. In most situations, this feedback generates a compelling case for additional reinforcement. This is particularly helpful for application evaluation, where the barriers and impediments to learning transfer are analyzed in a detailed study.

Improve Management Support for Learning and Development

Managers at the middle and top level in the organization often do not support learning and development for a variety of reasons. Sometimes they do not see value from these efforts in terms that they appreciate and understand. Evaluation data, particularly showing the application, impact, and even ROI, can provide convincing evidence for these managers to enhance support for learning and development in the future. Probably no more important reason for using evaluation data is to provide it to managers to build support and commitment—but only if it is data that they appreciate and desire, typically application, impact, and ROI data.

Improve Satisfaction With Stakeholders

Various stakeholders are involved in implementing learning and development programs. The next chapter provides some detail about how to get these various stakeholders involved. Evaluation data gives them a sense of the success of the program. In essence, they become more satisfied with a program when they see the value that it is adding. Application and impact data is particularly helpful for these stakeholders so that they can see that learning is actually making a difference in the organization.

Recognize and Reward Participants

The most critical stakeholder in learning and development is the actual participant who must learn, apply, and achieve results if the program is to add value. When this occurs at the rate and amount that is desired, the participants should be recognized for their efforts and perhaps even rewarded. When participants excel, in terms of their application and desired impact of learning and development on the job, they should be rewarded. Evaluation data provides this important clarification of the role of the participant, giving the credit to the group who actually achieved the success—the participants involved in learning and development processes.

Justify or Enhance Budget

In today's economic environment, an important reason for developing evaluation data is to show the value of learning and development. In tough economic times, learning and development staff can use evaluation to justify an existing budget or enhance the current budget. This use of data can only be accomplished if the evaluation is pushed to the business impact or ROI level. This way, executives approving budgets can clearly see the connection between learning and development and value added to the organization. In many case situations, the learning and development staff evaluates significant projects to enhance budgets in times when other budgets are being cut. Conversely, there are many examples where learning and development budgets are reduced because no studies are available to show the actual value.

Develop Norms and Standards

For evaluations that you repeat often, it may be helpful to develop standard data items and norms from the data. Norms are a way to compare one program to previous programs, the past performance of the current program, or even the same program in other organizations. Norms are important with reaction and satisfaction levels of evaluation but are gaining acceptance as benchmarking data for learning and application. Many organizations use consistent questions and compare responses in benchmarking efforts. Technology enables the development of norms across the organization and for the learning and development staff to set expectations around the norms.

Reduce Costs

Evaluation data can show how efficiencies can be generated with adjustments in the design, development, and delivery of a learning and development program. For example, asking participants how the same skills and knowledge could be acquired with an alternative process often provides important insights into ways to save costs. Asking how the particular program could be improved or how success could be enhanced provides useful information for making cost-effective adjustments. For example, a two-day program could be converted into two hours of e-learning, one day of facilitation and two hours of coaching. This transition could result in tremendous savings for a program offered many times. In many situations, evaluation data is used to drive changes that usually result in conserving budgets or reducing expenditures.

Market Learning and Development Programs

When participants have an option of attending, evaluation data can provide a convincing case to get them involved. Evaluation data can show how others have reacted to and used the knowledge and skills from the learning and development program. In essence, the participants, through evaluation data, show the advantages of being involved.

Marketing materials can be designed to let others know about the particular program. Included in the marketing material should be evaluation data demonstrating the success of the program, thereby adding an extra dimension to marketing by enticing individuals to become involved in, or to send others to, the program based on outcomes, not content. This marketing concept can only be developed if you collect data to show application, impact, and even ROI. In essence, this data provides a strategic marketing focus for learning and development, moving from the position of trying to sell learning and development to making learning and development attractive because of its value proposition.

Expand Implementation to Other Areas

One of the most profitable uses of evaluation data is to make a convincing case to implement a learning solution in other areas—if the same need is there. When a pilot program offered in one division shows a substantial contribution by adding tremendous value to the organization, a compelling case to implement it in other areas can be made, but only if a needs assessment or performance analysis has indicated the same need in that area.

Previously, the decision to expand had been made with qualitative data, often based on reaction to the program or the appearance of materials or content of the program. Evaluation data showing application, impact, and ROI can provide a more convincing case for this implementation moving to results-based decision making.

Monitoring Improvements

The use of evaluation data is limitless, and the options for providing data to various target audiences are vast. Table 6-2 shows each of the uses of

data described in this chapter with its linkage to the various levels of evaluation. This way, you can see how valuable the different levels can be in terms of driving improvement in the organization.

To ensure that data is applied to its intended use, it may be helpful to draft project plans or follow-up actions to help track improvements that have been made. For example, if a redesign is needed based on the evaluation data, it may be helpful to see if redesign has actually occurred. In some cases, this type of data should be provided to various stakeholders and, in some cases, even to participants themselves. They may need to understand that the evaluation is actually serving a purpose. The specific types of follow-up mechanism may vary, and several options are available. This final step may be the most important part of the process.

Final Thoughts

This chapter presented the final part in the evaluation process: communicating results and using data to drive improvement. If this step is not taken

Table 6-2. Matching strategies with levels of data.

Strategy	Appropriate Level of Data				
	1	2	3	4	5
Adjust Program Design	✓	✓			
Improve Program Delivery	✓	✓			
Influence Application and Impact			✓	✓	
Enhance Reinforcement for Learning			✓		
Improve Management Support for Learning and Development			✓	✓	
Improve Satisfaction With Stakeholders			✓	✓	✓
Recognize and Reward Participants		✓	✓	✓	
Justify or Enhance Budget				✓	✓
Develop Norms and Standards	✓	✓	✓		
Reduce Costs		✓	✓	✓	✓
Market Learning and Development Programs	✓		✓	✓	✓
Expand Implementation to Other Areas				✓	✓

seriously, the full impact of the results cannot be realized. The chapter began with general principles for communicating program results. The various target audiences were discussed with an emphasis on the executive group because of its importance. This chapter also suggested an organizational format for a detailed evaluation report and presented information about the most commonly used media for communicating program results.

Finally, this chapter presented a variety of uses of evaluation data, enabling the learning and development staff to plan the actual use of the data as it is presented to the various groups. A full array of possibilities exists to translate the communication into action.

Part Three

Making Evaluation Work in Your Organization

Method goes far to prevent trouble in business:
for it makes the task easy, hinders confusion, saves
abundance of time, and instructs those that have business
depending, both what to do and what to hope.

—John Greenleaf Whittier (1807–1892)

7

Improving Management Support

· ·

Lack of support for learning and evaluation is a serious and universal problem. A lack of strong management support can thwart an otherwise successful learning solution. Because job-related learning has little chance of being effective without manager support, some studies estimate that as much as 80 percent of what is taught in a program is not used. The principal culprit for the lack of utilization is the management group (Broad, 1997). The problem can be serious enough in some organizations to cause the ultimate demise of the learning and development function.

When discussing ways to improve support and involvement, there is little distinction between improving support for learning and improving support for evaluation. The techniques are the same. This chapter explores a variety of techniques to enhance support for learning and development *and* evaluation. Two key strategies are explored in more detail: building partnerships and conducting a special workshop for managers.

· ·

Why Managers Don't Always Support Learning

Managers are sometimes reluctant to support learning for a variety of reasons. Some reasons are valid, but others are based on misunderstandings about the learning and development function and its impact in the organization. An analysis of the current level of support usually reveals the most common problems, which are outlined below.

No Results

Managers are not convinced that job-related learning adds value in terms they understand and appreciate. They do not see programs producing results in ways to help them reach their objectives. Managers are rarely asked, "Is this learning program working for you?" or "Is it adding value to your department?" Learning and development professionals deserve much of the blame for this situation. The effectiveness of learning all too often is determined by the reactions of participants and measures of learning during the program. Managers need more application and impact data.

Too Costly

Managers perceive training as a double or triple cost. The direct cost for learning and development ultimately is taken from the operating profits and sometimes charged to their department. They also see formal learning programs as taking employees away from their jobs, which results in a loss of productivity. They experience a personal cost for finding ways to get the job done while an employee is involved in the program. They must rearrange work schedules to meet deadlines, find new ways to meet service requirements, redistribute the workload, or secure a replacement. In some cases, the method of recording time when employees attend formal learning programs reinforces this notion if the time off the job is labeled "nonproductive." Unfortunately, this sends an important and sometimes negative message throughout the organization. Because double and triple cost perceptions are unfounded, managers must be persuaded of the true cost of learning.

No Input

Managers don't support learning because they are not offered an opportunity for input into the process. They are not asked for their views on the content or focus of a program during needs assessment or program formulation. They are rarely provided objectives that link learning to job performance improvements or business results. Without input, managers do not develop a sense of ownership for learning and development.

No Relevance

Managers have little reason to believe that learning programs have job relevance or will help their department or work unit. They see content descriptions that bear little resemblance to work-related issues. They hear comments about learning activities that are unrelated to current challenges faced by the team. Managers have many requests and demands for resources. They quickly eliminate the unnecessary frills and what they perceive to be busy work. No relevance equals no need, which equals no priority and eventually leads to no support.

No Involvement

Managers do not support learning because they are not actively involved in the process in any meaningful way. Even in some of the best organizations, the manager's role is severely restricted or limited, sometimes by design and other times by default. To build respect for the learning and development function, managers should have some type of active involvement in the process. This involvement ranges from reinforcing learning for programs for their employees to actually delivering part of a program as a facilitator.

No Time

Managers don't have the time to support formal learning and development. They are busy with ever-increasing demands on their time. When establishing daily priorities, the specific actions necessary to show support for learning just don't make it to the top of the list. Consequently, nothing happens. Managers often perceive that requests for increased support always require additional time. In reality, many supportive actions *do not* require much time; it's often a matter of perception.

No Preparation

Sometimes managers lack the skills necessary to provide reinforcement to participants after they attend programs. Although they may be willing to offer support, managers may not know how to provide feedback, respond to questions, guide participants through specific issues, or help achieve results with programs. Specific skills are needed to provide effective reinforcement, just as specific skills are required for planning, budgeting, delegating, and negotiating.

Lack of Knowledge About Learning and Development

Managers are not always aware of the nature and scope of learning and development. Perhaps they know that it's a legitimate function necessary to equip new employees with specific skills and knowledge required for the job, but, beyond that, they are not fully aware of what learning and development can provide for the organization. They do not fully understand the different steps involved from needs assessment to development, delivery, and evaluation. They see bits and pieces of the process but may not know how they are integrated to create an effective process. It is difficult for managers to support a process they don't fully understand.

No Requirements

Finally, managers do not support learning and development because they are not sure what they are supposed to do. If the only request from the learning and development department is to allow participants to attend a program, that is all they will do. The learning and development staff usually creates this problem because they don't make the contact; they do not communicate directly with the operating managers to let them know what is needed and what managers must do to make the process work.

Collectively, these reasons for not supporting learning and evaluation equate to challenges for learning and development departments and represent opportunities for managers. If the issues are not addressed in an effective way, management support will not exist, transfer of learning will be diminished, and, consequently, results will be severely limited or nonexistent.

Improving Commitment and Support

Management's actions and perceptions significantly affect the success of learning and development programs, as well as their impact on the organization. This influence is critical in the workplace, even beyond program development and delivery. Although the learning and development staff members may have little direct control over some of these factors, they can exert a tremendous amount of influence on them. Table 7-1 lists the key actions needed by the management team.

Table 7-1. Comparison of key management actions.

Management Action	Target Group	Scope	Payoff
Management commitment	Top executives	All programs	Very high
Management support	Middle managers, first-level supervisors	Usually several programs	High
Management reinforcement	First-level managers	Specific programs	Moderate
Management involvement	All levels of managers	Specific programs	Moderate

Several terms used in table 7-1 need some additional explanation (Phillips, Stone & Phillips, 2001). *Management commitment, management support, management involvement, management reinforcement, maintenance of behavior,* and *transfer of learning* are overlapping and sometimes confusing terms. *Management commitment* usually refers to the top-management group and includes its pledge or promise to allocate resources and support to the learning and development effort. *Management support* refers to the actions of the entire management group and reflects the group's attitude toward the learning and development process and staff. The major emphasis is on middle and first-line management. Their supportive actions can tremendously impact the success of programs. *Management involvement* refers to the extent to which executives and managers are actively engaged in the learning process in addition to participating in programs. Because *management commitment, support,* and *involvement* have similar meanings, these terms are often used interchangeably in current literature.

Management reinforcement, maintenance of behavior, and *transfer of learning* also have similar meanings. *Management reinforcement* refers to actions designed to reward or encourage a desired behavior. The goal is to increase the probability of the behavior occurring after a participant attends a program. *Maintenance of behavior* refers to the organization's actions to maintain a change in behavior on the job after the program is completed. *Transfer of learning* refers to the extent to which the learned behavior and knowledge from the program is used on the job.

The Management Support Dilemma

You've just read about more than a few compelling reasons why management does not always support learning and evaluation. To overcome these barriers, it is necessary to first assess the current status of management support, and then take steps to increase management's commitment to learning and evaluation, build management support, improve reinforcement systems, and encourage management involvement. These processes are described more fully in the sections that follow.

Assess the Current Status

A preliminary step to improve support is to assess the current level of support from the management group. A tool for this assessment is presented in appendix A. The instrument addresses 30 important issues that collectively measure the degree of management support for the learning and development function. The target group for assessment may be any management group (division, plant, corporate, or region, at middle management or senior level). High scores on this instrument indicate a strong, supportive environment. Low scores indicate serious problems, signaling a need for actions to improve support. An analysis of scores is also included at the end of the appendix.

Bolster Commitment

Commitment is necessary to secure the resources for a viable learning and development effort. Table 7-2 shows the 10 general areas of emphasis for strong top-management commitment. These 10 areas are critical to any successful learning and development effort.

Now for the big question: How can top-management commitment increase? The amount of commitment varies with the size or nature of the organization. Quite often the extent of commitment is fixed in the organization before the learning and development manager becomes involved with the function. It usually depends on how the function evolved, top management's attitude and philosophy toward learning and development, and the way the function is administered.

The key to the solution of increasing commitment lies in the results. Top-management commitment usually increases when programs obtain desired results. As figure 7-1 illustrates, this is a relentless cycle because commitment is necessary to build effective programs from which results can be obtained. And when results are obtained, commitment increases. *Nothing is more convincing to a*

Table 7-2. The 10 commitments of top management.

For strong top-management learning and development commitment, the top executive should:

1. Develop or approve a mission for the learning and development function.
2. Allocate the necessary funds for successful learning and development programs.
3. Allow employees time to participate in learning and development programs.
4. Become actively involved in learning and development programs and require others to do the same.
5. Support the learning and development effort and ask other managers to do the same.
6. Position the learning and development function in a visible and high-level place on the organization chart.
7. Require that each learning and development program be evaluated in some way.
8. Insist that learning and development programs be cost effective and require supporting data.
9. Set an example for self-development, leadership, and continuous learning.
10. Create an atmosphere of open communication with the learning and development manager.

group of top executives than programs with measurable results they can understand. When a program is proposed, additional funding may be based solely on the results the program is expected to produce.

In addition to providing results, several actions or strategies can help increase commitment from management. When they are actively involved in programs, managers become more deeply committed to learning and development. This involvement, which can occur in almost every phase of the learning process, reflects a strong cooperative management effort to use human resources effectively.

A professional, competent staff can help improve commitment. Where the achievement of excellence is the goal of many professional groups, it should be a mandate for the learning and development department. The staff must be perceived as professional in all actions, including welcoming

Figure 7-1. The results commitment cycle.

criticism, adjusting to the changing needs of the organization, maintaining productive relationships with other staff, and setting the example for others.

Top executives are more inclined to provide additional funds to a staff who understands the business and is willing to help the organization reach its goals. Comprehensive knowledge of the organization's primary businesses is a key ingredient in building respect and credibility with the management group.

The learning and development department must communicate needs to top managers to help them understand that learning is an integral part of the organization. When top management understands the results-based process, they usually respond with additional commitment.

The staff should take a visible role, preferably alongside key managers, as they work to solve operational problems. Top executives want staff members who are truly involved, who have a hands-on philosophy and a desire to be in the midst of the action. Top management usually supports those who meet this challenge.

The learning and development department should avoid being narrowly focused. Programs should not be confined to those mandated by regulations, laws, or organizational necessities. The staff must be regarded as problem solvers or performance enhancers. A progressive staff is perceived as versatile, flexible, and resourceful, and is utilized in a variety of situations to help make a contribution to organizational success.

Finally, the learning and development department must have a practical approach to program design, development, and implementation. An approach focusing on theories and philosophical ideas may be perceived as not contributing to the organization.

Build Management Support

Before discussing techniques to improve support for programs, it is appropriate to present the concept of ideal management support. Ideal support occurs when a manager reacts in the following ways to a participant's involvement in a learning and development program:

- encourages participants to be involved in programs
- volunteers personal services or resources to assist with learning and development
- outlines expectations prior to the program and details what changes should take place or what tasks the participant should accomplish after completing the program
- reinforces in any of several ways the behavior change resulting from the program
- helps to determine the results achieved from the program
- rewards participants who achieve outstanding accomplishments with the program
- provides unsolicited positive comments about the success of programs.

This level of support for a program represents utopia for the learning and development department. Support is necessary before and after the program is conducted. Effective actions prior to a program can significantly influence the success of the program and application on the job.

Mid- and first-level managers are important to program success. The degree to which managers support programs is based on the value they place on learning. To improve management support, the learning and development staff must regularly show the results achieved from programs, help managers assume more responsibility for learning and development, explore ways to increase the level of involvement, and teach them about the learning and development cycle. One key strategy for accomplishing this is a special workshop for managers, described later in this chapter.

Improve Reinforcement

The importance of management reinforcement as an integral part of the process cannot be overstated. Too often participants return from a program to find roadblocks to successfully applying what they learned. Faced with these obstacles, even some of the best participants revert to old habits and forget most of what they learned in the program. In fact, regardless of how well the program is designed and presented, unless it is reinforced on the job, most of the effectiveness is lost. This reinforcement should come from the immediate manager of the participant.

The reason for this problem lies in the nature of change and learning. When learning a skill, participants go through a frustrating period when the skill does not feel natural and is not producing the desired results. This period represents a decline in results and is difficult for most participants. However, those who persist gain the expected reward from the new behavior. If the participant continues the new behavior or skill, that behavior will eventually feel more natural and performance improves. Without proper reinforcement, particularly during the time when results decline, participants may abandon the acquired skills. They may revert to the familiar old ways of behavior.

Although self-reinforcement and peer reinforcement are helpful, participants' immediate managers are the primary focus for reinforcement efforts. An immediate manager can exert significant influence on the participant's behavior by providing reinforcement in the following ways:

- helping the participant diagnose problems to determine if new skills are needed
- discussing possible alternatives for handling specific situations and acting as a coach to help the participant apply the skills
- encouraging the participant to use the skills frequently
- serving as a role model for the proper use of the skills
- providing positive rewards to the participant when the skills are successfully used.

Each of these activities reinforces the objectives of the program. In some organizations, managers are required to provide this level of reinforcement.

Job expectations and job descriptions are adjusted to reflect reinforcement processes. In other organizations, reinforcement is encouraged and supported by top executives.

Improve Management Involvement

Management involvement in learning and development is not a new process. Organizations have practiced it successfully for many years. Management should be involved in most key decisions of the learning and development department. Although almost as many opportunities exist for management's involvement in learning and development as there are steps in a learning systems model, management input and active participation generally only occur in the key steps and most significant programs. The following sections cover the primary vehicles for obtaining management involvement.

Advisory Committees. Many organizations develop committees to enhance line management involvement in the learning and development process. These committees, which act in an advisory capacity to the department, may have other names, such as councils or people development boards. As shown in table 7-3, committees can be developed for individual programs, specific functions, or multiple functions.

Learning and Development Taskforces. Another potential area for management involvement is through the use of a taskforce. A taskforce consists of a group of employees (usually management) who are charged with the responsibility for developing a learning and development program.

Taskforces are particularly useful for programs beyond the scope of the learning and development staff's capability. A taskforce can considerably reduce the time required to develop a new program. In a lease-financing firm, for example, a group of managers served on a taskforce to design and implement a talent management program. The group had ownership of the program.

Table 7-3. Types of committees for increasing management involvement in learning and development.

Responsible for:	Examples:
Individual Program	• New Team Leader Development Program Committee • Account Executives' Training Program Committee • Product Knowledge Course Committee • Underwriter Training Committee
Specific Function	• Sales Development Committee • Nurse Development Committee • Six Sigma Training Committee • IT Training Committee
Multiple Functions	• Management Development Committee • Faculty Development Committee • Skills Training Committee • Compliance Training Committee

Managers as Experts. Managers may provide expertise for program design, development, or implementation. Subject matter experts (SMEs) provide a valuable and necessary service while developing attachment to the program. As an example, at a refrigerator manufacturing plant, managers served as experts in a major job redesign project. The traditional assembly line was replaced with a work cell arrangement. The expertise of the managers was critical to program success.

Managers as Participants. Managerial participation can range from attending the program to auditing a portion of the program. In a telecommunications company, managers participated in a diversity awareness program designed for all employees. This participation was helpful to achieve success with the program. Be aware, however, participation may not be feasible for all types of programs, such as specialized projects designed for only a few individuals.

Program Leaders. A powerful way to improve managers and professionals is to use them as program leaders. Facilitation builds ownership. In a large hospital chain, managers served as facilitators in employee meetings designed to prevent sexual harassment complaints.

Involving Managers in Evaluation. Another area in which managers can be involved in the learning and development process is in the evaluation of programs. Although management is sometimes involved in assessing the ultimate outcome of learning programs, this process focuses directly on evaluation at different times and activities. Several ways in which the learning and development team can involve managers in evaluation are:

- Invite managers to participate in focus groups about program success.
- Ask managers to collect application and impact data.
- Review program success data with managers.
- Ask managers to interpret results.
- Convene managers to share overall results.
- Ask managers to communicate data, including impact and ROI.

Involving managers and showing them how evaluation can work increases commitment and support for learning and evaluation.

New Roles for Managers. These approaches are primary ways to involve managers in the learning and development process when the focus is on achieving results. Many other ways are available in which managers can be involved. In essence, these types of management involvement define new learning and development roles for managers in an organization. In these roles, managers may

- coordinate or organize learning programs
- participate in needs assessment
- provide expertise for program design
- facilitate learning and development
- reinforce learning and development
- evaluate learning, application, and business impact
- drive actions for improvement based on program evaluation data.

Ideally, managers should assume these key roles, and the learning and development staff should communicate the program's results frequently. Collectively, these actions increase support and commitment and also enhance input from each learning role. Table 7-4 shows the opportunities for

management involvement in the various steps of a results-based process.

Key Strategy: Developing Partnerships With Managers

Building a partnership with key managers is one of the most powerful ways to increase management involvement and support. A partnership relationship can assume any of three basic levels of formality. Although these three levels of formality are distinct, a learning and development department can move through all these different levels as the partnering process matures and achieves success (Bell & Shea, 1998).

In some organizations, the relationship is informal, loosely defined, and ill structured. By design, these organizations do not want to develop the relationship to a formal level but continue to refine it informally.

In other organizations, the process is formalized to the extent that specific activities are planned with

Table 7-4. Manager involvement opportunities.

Step in the Results-Based Process	Opportunity for Manager Involvement	Most Appropriate Strategy
Conduct Analysis	High	Taskforce
Develop Measurement and Evaluation System	Moderate	Advisory committee
Establish Program Objectives	High	Advisory committee
Develop Program	Moderate	Taskforce
Implement Program	High	Program leader
Monitor Costs	Low	Expert input
Collect and Analyze Data	Moderate	Expert input
Interpret Data and Draw Conclusions	High	Expert input
Communicate Results	Moderate	Manager as participant

specific individuals, all for the purpose of improving relationships. The quality of the relationships is discussed, and assessments typically are taken to gauge progress.

In still other situations, the process is very formal. Individuals are discreetly identified for relationship improvement, and a written plan is developed for each individual. Sometimes a contract is developed with a particular manager. Assessments are routinely taken, and progress is reported formally.

Regardless of the degree of formality, for effective relationship building, the learning and development staff must take the initiative to organize, plan, and measure the progress. The staff must *want* to develop the relationship. Rarely do key managers approach the learning staff to nurture these relationships. In some organizations, key managers don't want to develop relationships because of the concern about the time it may take to work through these issues. They may see no need for the relationship and consider it a waste of time. To overcome this barrier requires the learning and development staff to properly assess the situation, plan strategies, and take appropriate actions—routinely and consistently—to ensure that the process is working.

For this process to be effective, the executive or manager responsible for the learning and development function must take the lead and involve others as appropriate and necessary. The direction must come from the top. Although this responsibility cannot be delegated, it can involve many other members of the learning and development staff, if not all. There are two critical issues—the steps to build the partner relationship and the principles involved in developing and nurturing the relationship (Mariotti, 1996). The next sections discuss both issues.

The first, and perhaps the most important, issue deals with the specific steps necessary to develop a partner relationship. Second, a set of principles must be followed when building and nurturing the relationship

Fourteen Steps to a Partner Relationship

Building a partner relationship between management and the learning and development function involves a series of steps:

1. Assess the current status of partnership relationships. The first course of action is to determine the current condition by assessing the status of these 10 issues: choice of partners, willingness to become a partner, trust with partner, character and ethics, culture fit, common goals and interests, information sharing among partners, fair sharing of both risks and rewards among the partners, degree of commitment to the partnership, and value given and received. Learning and development staff members should determine present status on each of these specific issues, using an appropriate scale. This assessment provides information for planning and provides an opportunity to determine progress in the future.

2. Identify key individuals for a partnership relationship. Building a partnership works best when the focus is on a few individuals.

3. Learn the business. An effective partnership relationship cannot be developed unless the learning and development staff member understands the operational and strategic issues of the organization.

4. Consider a written plan. The process is often more focused when it is written with specific details for each manager.

5. Offer assistance to solve problems. The learning and development staff should support managers and provide assistance to solve problems.

6. Show results of programs. When results are achieved, quick communication with managers is important to demonstrate to them how a program achieved success. In addition, the results achieved from other

programs should be communicated to these key managers.

7. Publicize partners' accomplishments and successes. Every opportunity to give proper credit to the accomplishments of the partner should be taken.

8. Ask the partner to review needs. Whenever a needs assessment is requested or undertaken as part of an overall macro-level assessment, the partner should be asked to review the information and confirm, or add to, the needs.

9. Have the partner serve on an advisory committee. A helpful approach to provide guidance and direction to the learning and development staff or a particular program is to establish an advisory committee.

10. Shift responsibility to the partner. Although the success of learning and development rests with multiple stakeholders, the primary responsibility for learning and developing employees must lie with the management group.

11. Invite input from the partner about key plans and programs. Routinely, key managers should be asked to provide information about issues such as needs assessment, program design, new technology, program delivery, and follow-up evaluation.

12. Ask the partner to review program objectives, content, and delivery mechanisms. As a routine activity, these managers should review objectives, content, and planned delivery for each new program or major redesign in their individual areas.

13. Invite the partner to conduct or coordinate a program or portion of a program.

14. Review progress and re-plan strategy. Periodically the partnership process should be reviewed to check progress and readjust the strategy, if necessary.

Key Principles for the Partnership

As the specific steps are undertaken to develop a partnership with management, it is important to preserve the nature and quality of the relationship. Several essential principles serve as an operating framework to develop, nurture, and refine this critical relationship. Table 7-5 lists key principles, which should be integrated into each step.

Key Strategy: Manager Workshop

Another effective approach to secure increased management involvement and support for evaluation is to conduct a workshop for managers. Varying in duration from a half-day to two days, a practical workshop on the manager's role in learning and

---

Table 7-5. Key principles when developing a partnership relationship.

1. Have patience and persistence throughout the process.
2. Follow win-win opportunities for both parties.
3. Deal with problems and conflicts quickly.
4. Share information regularly and purposefully.
5. Always be honest and display the utmost integrity in all the transactions.
6. Keep high standards of professionalism in each interaction.
7. Give credit and recognition to the partner routinely.
8. Take every opportunity to explain, inform, and educate.
9. Involve managers in as many activities as possible.

development can shape critical skills and change perceptions to enhance support for learning and development. Managers leave the workshop with an improved perception of the impact of learning and a clearer understanding of their roles in the learning and performance improvement process. More important, they often have a renewed commitment to make learning work in their organization.

Because of the critical need in management development, this workshop should be required for all managers, unless they have previously demonstrated strong support for the learning and development function. Because of this requirement, it is essential for top executives to be supportive of this workshop and, in some cases, take an active role in conducting it. To tailor the program to specific organizational needs, a brief needs assessment may be necessary to determine the specific focus and areas of emphasis for the program.

Workshop Design Issues

Although the target audience for a manager workshop is usually middle-level managers, the target group is likely to vary from organization to organization. In some organizations, the target may be first-level managers, and in others, the target may be second-level managers. Three important questions help determine the proper audience:

- Which group has the most direct influence on the learning and development function?
- Which management group is causing serious problems with lack of management support?
- Which group has the need to understand learning and development evaluation so it can influence learning transfer?

Oftentimes, the answer to all these questions is middle-level managers.

This workshop should be conducted early in the management development process before nonsupportive habits become established. When this program is implemented throughout the organiza-

tion, it is best to start with high-level managers and work down the organization. If possible, a version of the program should be a part of a traditional management training program provided to team leaders when they are promoted into managerial positions.

Checklists, exercises, case studies, and skill practices are all helpful in this workshop to illustrate and reinforce concepts necessary in this workshop. As with any management training program, active involvement is essential. Case studies help illustrate the problems that occur when learning is not supported by management.

The material used in this workshop must be practical and easily understandable to the management group. It must be free of typical adult learning jargon. It should be targeted to the specific needs of managers and presented from the perspective of the manager. "Nice to know" topics should be avoided.

Because of its importance, the most effective facilitators who have credibility with the management team must conduct this program. Sometimes external consultants, who enjoy an excellent reputation in the learning and development field, are tapped to conduct such workshops.

Selling Top Management

Convincing top management to require a management workshop is sometimes a difficult task. Three approaches should be considered:

1. Discuss and illustrate the consequences of inadequate management support for training, learning, and performance. For example, the statistics are staggering in terms of wasted time and money.

2. Show how current support is lacking. A recent evaluation of an internal learning program can often reveal the barriers to successful application of learning. Lack of management support is often the main reason, which brings the issue close to home.

3. Demonstrate how money can be saved and results can be achieved by having managers

more involved in the learning and development process.

The endorsement of the top management group is very important. In some organizations, top managers actually attend the program to explore firsthand what is involved and what they must do to make learning successful. At a minimum, top management should support the program by signing memos describing the program or by approving policy statements for required participation.

Workshop Content

The program can be developed in separate modules allowing managers to be exempted from certain modules based on their previous knowledge or experience with the topic. The following sections offer some ideas about modules that could be included in a management workshop.

The Overall Importance of Learning. After completing this module, managers should perceive learning and development as a critical function in their organization and be able to describe how the process contributes to strategic and operational objectives. During this module, managers become convinced that learning and development is a mainstream responsibility that is gaining in importance and influence in the organizations. Data from the organization is presented to show the full scope of learning and development in the organization. Tangible evidence of top management commitment is presented in a form of memos, directives, and policies signed by the CEO or other appropriate top executive.

The Impact of Learning and Development. After completing this module, managers will be able to identify the steps to measure the impact of learning and development on important output variables. Reports and studies should be presented, showing impact using measures such as productivity, quality, cost, cycle times, and customer satisfaction. If internal reports are not available, other success stories or case studies from other organizations can be used.

Learning and Development Process. After completing this module, managers should be able to describe how the learning process works in their organization and understand each critical step of the cycle from needs assessment to ROI calculation. Managers are often reluctant to support activities or processes they do not fully understand. During this module, managers are made aware of the effort that goes into developing a learning program and their role in each step of the process. This module should include a short case, illustrating all the steps of program design, implementation, and evaluation.

Responsibility for HRD. After completing this module, managers should be able to list their specific responsibilities for learning and development. Defining who is responsible for formal learning and development is important to the success of the process. Managers can see how they can influence learning and development results and the degree of responsibility they must assume in the future. A case study can illustrate the consequences of managers neglecting their responsibilities or failing to follow up where learning is concerned.

An exercise in this module reveals the perceptions of support offered by managers when compared to the level of support perceived by their direct reports. Data from a follow-up study is presented to show the profile of manager behavior after a participant attends a formal learning program. The same profile of behavior is collected from the managers and compared to the input from participants. Table 7-6 shows the two sets of actual data from a reaction questionnaire for a program designed for first-level managers.

As table 7-6 demonstrates, there is a marked difference in manager behavior as perceived by the participant who attended the program and the manager's own perception of actual support. Such differences are typical. This example emphasizes the following major points:

- Managers tend to overrate the effectiveness and helpfulness of their support.

Table 7-6. Management's support of learning: contrasting perceptions.

Participants' Responses Concerning Managers' Support:	
My manager told me to forget what I've learned; it doesn't work here.	12%
My manager said to be very careful about using the material; it may not work here.	22%
My manager said nothing.	53%
My manager said that I should (could) try to use what I've learned.	8%
My manager said that he/she expects me to use this material.	5%
My manager coached and supported me through the application of the material.	0%
Managers' Responses Concerning Their Support:	
I told him/her to forget what was learned; it won't work here.	0%
I told him/her to be very careful about using the material; it may not work here.	0%
I said nothing.	4%
I told him/her to try (consider trying) to use what was learned.	11%
I said that I expected him/her to use the material.	36%
I coached and supported him/her through the application of the material.	49%

- Participants usually rate manager support as being ineffective.
- Management support is an extremely important issue in transferring learning to the job.

Active Involvement. One of the most important ways to enhance manager support for learning and development is to get the manager actively involved in the process. After completing this module, managers will actually commit to one or more ways of active involvement in the future. Table 7-7 shows 12 ways for managers to become involved. The information in this table was presented to managers in a workshop offered at one company. Managers were asked to commit to at least one area of involvement.

After these areas are fully explained and discussed at the workshop, each manager is asked to select one or more ways in which he or she will be involved in learning and development in the future. A commitment to sign up for at least one involvement role is required. If used properly, these commitments provide a rich source of input and assistance from the management group.

Other Workshop Features

Some common variations to the workshop format and presentation are these:

- The program is held offsite to take participants away from job pressures and distractions. This change of scenery can help them to focus directly on the workshop material without interruption.
- Prework is required. Having participants complete the survey and read cases in advance can be helpful.
- Cross-functional groups can help participants see the learning and development function from different perspectives within the organization.
- The workshop is an excellent opportunity to present impact studies or other data that shows the business results from learning and development.
- Reference materials are provided.

Table 7-7. Management's involvement in learning and development.

The following are areas for present and future involvement in the learning and development process. Please check your areas of planned involvement.

	In Your Area	Outside Your Area
Attend a program designed for your staff	☐	☐
Provide input on a needs analysis	☐	☐
Serve on an HRD advisory committee	☐	☐
Provide input on a program design	☐	☐
Serve as a subject matter expert	☐	☐
Serve on a taskforce to develop a program	☐	☐
Volunteer to evaluate an external learning and development program	☐	☐
Assist in the selection of a vendor-supplied learning and development program	☐	☐
Provide reinforcement to your employees after they attend a learning program	☐	☐
Coordinate a learning and development program	☐	☐
Assist in program evaluation or follow-up	☐	☐
Conduct a portion of the program as a facilitator	☐	☐

Payoff of the Workshop

This workshop should help to eliminate many of the barriers to successful learning and development caused by lack of management support. As a result of the workshop, there should be increases in supportive actions as measured in follow-up surveys. Many follow-up evaluations collect data on the extent and level of management support after participants attend formal programs.

The individual manager's commitments for active involvement are tangible evidence of success because the involvement can be measured by the follow-through on planned actions. Also, participation in all learning programs should improve for programs involving voluntary attendance. When managers fully understand the learning process and their role in it, they gain a renewed determination to make it work. Managers' attitudes toward learning and development should be more positive as measured on a post-program assessment, using the same instrument as presented in the pre-program assessment (appendix A).

Final Thoughts

This chapter explored the critical influence of the management group on the success of evaluation. It is impossible for a learning or performance improvement to be successful without the positive and supportive influence of the management group. The target groups for action include the top managers who must demonstrate their commitment to the evaluation through resource allocation. Middle managers who support learning in a variety of ways are ideal targets for partnership relationships with the staff. First-level managers must support and reinforce the objectives of the programs. Without such reinforcement, programs will not be as successful as they should be.

This chapter outlined a variety of strategies to work effectively with all of these groups. Specific emphasis was placed on two key strategies: developing partnerships and conducting a special workshop for managers.

8

Overcoming Resistance to Evaluation

•••••••••••••••••••••••••••••••••••••••

The best designed model or technique is worthless unless it is effectively integrated into the organization. The simplest, most methodical process will fail even in the best organizations if it is not fully supported by those who should make it work. Learning and development staff members and others closely associated with the implementation of evaluation must realize the benefits of evaluation, particularly when evaluating ROI. Sometimes, resistance appears in negative ways. For the most part, there is a rational argument as to why the resistance exists. Fundamentally, resistance to learning and development evaluation is much the same as resistance to any change process. This chapter explores the major resistance points and the actions you can take to remove or minimize resistance. These actions translate into a project plan for transition to a more comprehensive evaluation process. The chapter concludes with the actions needed to sustain the evaluation process and make it routine within the organization.

•••••••••••••••••••••••••••••••••••••••

Fear and Uncertainty = Resistance

Learning and development staff members and others closely associated with their programs usually resist evaluation for two reasons:

- anticipation of the time needed to implement the process
- concern about the consequences of the final outcomes.

These two fears are often manifested for good reason. Implementing a comprehensive evaluation takes time, effort, and leadership. The fear of having another thing on the to-do list can be daunting. The fear of poorly designed or implemented programs being "exposed" can lead to resistance. The fear of discovering that a particular program really did cost too much can be unsettling. Therefore, the fundamental basis for resistance is fear or uncertainty.

Before reading further, however, you can assess the current level of evaluation resistance in your organization by using the assessment presented in exercise 8-1.

The 10 items listed in the exercise represent the top 10 resistors to measurement and evaluation often expressed by stakeholders. Each is briefly described here:

- *I don't have time for additional measurement and evaluation.* Learning and development staff members and other stakeholders are often fully challenged with current responsibilities. Measurement and evaluation often require additional tasks and responsibilities, taxing an already busy schedule. Few people want to add to their list of tasks unless they perceive the addition as an important benefit.
- *An unsuccessful evaluation project will reflect poorly on my performance.* If the data

---

Exercise 8-1. What is your organization's current level of evaluation resistance?

Rate the extent to which you agree with the following statements:
A rating of 1 = Strongly Disagree
A rating of 5 = Strongly Agree

	Strongly Disagree				Strongly Agree
	1	2	3	4	5
1. I do not have time for additional measurement and evaluation.	☐	☐	☐	☐	☐
2. An unsuccessful evaluation will reflect poorly on my performance.	☐	☐	☐	☐	☐
3. A negative ROI will kill my program.	☐	☐	☐	☐	☐
4. My budget will not allow for additional measurement and evaluation.	☐	☐	☐	☐	☐
5. Measurement and evaluation are not part of my job.	☐	☐	☐	☐	☐
6. I did not have input on this process.	☐	☐	☐	☐	☐
7. I do not understand this process.	☐	☐	☐	☐	☐
8. Our managers will not support this process.	☐	☐	☐	☐	☐
9. Data will be misused.	☐	☐	☐	☐	☐
10. The data is too subjective.	☐	☐	☐	☐	☐

If you scored:
10–25 = You like new challenges and are accepting of change.
21–30 = You go with the flow.
31–40 = You stress out and resist change.

collected shows that their part of the process is not working so well, learning and development staff members want to know the consequences. "Is my performance review influenced?" is often a silent question. Performance reviews often determine the opportunity for new assignments, promotions, or salary increases. Ideally, learning and development staff members, along with their managers and senior leaders, should view measurement and evaluation as a process improvement tool instead of a performance appraisal technique.

- *A negative ROI will kill my program.* This is an important concern when evaluation is elevated to the ROI level. Learning and development staff members fear that a negative ROI spells the end of a program that may ultimately add value, if some adjustments are made or if additional streams of benefits are included. These reluctant staff members sometimes miss the fact that other measures of program success, both qualitative and quantitative, are generated along with ROI to balance reporting of program success.

- *My budget will not allow for additional measurement and evaluation.* Additional costs can create a problem for an organization struggling to retain its present budget. There is a fear that additional funding will come at the expense of other processes, services, or products. With this view, the staff may ignore the payoff of a comprehensive evaluation process or the fact that a budget can be funded gradually with the savings generated by the process.

- *Measurement and evaluation are not a part of my job.* Many learning and development staff members have skills for specific duties, most of which have little to do with measurement and evaluation. Although the learning environment is changing, there is a reluctance to add to existing duties. "Job creep," as it is sometimes called, refers to

the slow progression of job responsibilities without additional pay, compensation, or recognition. Staff members may perceive measurement and evaluation duties as job creep.

- *I did not have any input regarding this process.* This concern is fundamental to any change effort. Individuals want to be involved in decisions affecting them and their work. If they are not involved, they fear it is a tool to be used against them or one that will be misused even in the best scenario. They want to have input on its development, when and how it will be used, and how the results will be used and communicated.

- *I do not understand this process.* Measurement and evaluation can be confusing. Much of the job preparation of learning and development staff members does not include formal skill building in measurement and evaluation. Consequently, there is a lack of understanding that breeds mistrust and fear. Many learning and development staff members are not motivated to learn such a process on their own.

- *Our managers will not support this process.* Because learning and development programs often lack proper support from the management team, the staff may assume that measurement and evaluation will fall in the same category. They immediately perceive that the management team will not provide data or use the results in any meaningful way. More important, managers will not provide funding for this type of activity.

- *Data will be misused.* Although staff members may realize that measurement and evaluation should be used for process improvement, they fear that others may not agree. There is a fear of data misuse, even beyond the scope of the learning and development staff. As managers and executives review data, the learning and development staff fear that the information will be misunderstood, misinterpreted, or used for political influence to gain support of programs.

■ *The data is too subjective.* Some fear the use of too much subjective data that is not fact based. These opinions are often formed in response to comments from casual observers of the process. These observers have inappropriately concluded that the process is based on a variety of subjective opinions.

These 10 issues cause resistance to any measurement and evaluation process. The resistance is amplified when the term ROI is used. The next section focuses on specific actions that can be taken to reduce these fears, clarify misunderstandings, and minimize the resistance for additional measurement and evaluation up to and including ROI.

Fearless Evaluation Implementation

Resistance to implementing a comprehensive measurement and evaluation process can be overcome by first recognizing that resistance is inevitable. Regardless of the reason, any type of change causes a flurry of questions, doubts, and fears. There may be legitimate reasons for resistance; however, it often exists for the wrong reasons. An initial step in overcoming resistance to implementing a comprehensive measurement and evaluation process is sorting out the reasons for the resistance and separating the myths from legitimate concerns. When legitimate barriers to implementation exist, minimizing or removing them altogether is the task.

As with any new process, effective implementation is the key to its success. Without it, even the best process will fail. This occurs when the new technique or tool is integrated into the routine framework. An off-the-shelf process will never be understood, supported, or improved. Specific steps and implementation criteria must be developed to ensure successful implementation.

As numerous evaluations are conducted, consistency is an important consideration. With consistency comes accuracy and reliability. Consistency is achieved through clearly defined processes and procedures each time evaluation is pursued. Proper implementation ensures that this occurs. Cost control is an issue in the implementation of measurement and evaluation. Implementation tasks must be completed efficiently as well as effectively to minimize costs, use time efficiently, and keep the process affordable.

The implementation necessary to overcome resistance covers a variety of areas. Figure 8-1 shows the building blocks to overcoming resistance. These building blocks serve as a framework to calm fears and remove or minimize barriers to implementation.

Identify a Champion

As a first step to overcome resistance, one or more individuals should be designated as the external champion. As with most change efforts, someone must take the lead for ensuring that the measurement and evaluation process is implemented successfully. This leader serves as a champion for evaluation. He or she understands the intent of evaluation, including ROI, and sees the vast potential for its contribution. More important, this leader is willing to show and teach others.

The evaluation leader is usually a member of the learning and development staff who has this responsibility full time in larger organizations or part time in smaller organizations. Typical job titles for a full-time leader are measurement manager, evaluation specialist, or measurement and evaluation advisor. Some organizations assign this responsibility to a team and empower them to lead the evaluation effort. Still, in others, the learning and development manager serves in this role.

Assign Roles and Responsibilities

Determining specific responsibilities is important to prevent the confusion created when individuals are unclear about their evaluation assignments.

Most responsibilities apply to two broad groups. The first group is the entire learning and

Figure 8-1. Building blocks for overcoming resistance.

Building Blocks			
	Remove the Barriers	Prepare Management Team	Report Progress
	Select Programs for Evaluation	Teach the Staff	Involve the Learning and Development Staff
	Revise Policies and Procedures	Develop a Project Plan	Establish Evaluation Targets
	Asses the Climate	Assign Roles and Responsibilities	Identify a Champion

development staff, those involved in designing, developing, delivering, coordinating, and supporting programs. Typical responsibilities include providing input on the design of instruments, planning a specific evaluation, collecting data, and interpreting the results. Specific responsibilities include

- ensuring that the needs assessment includes specific business impact measures
- developing specific learning, application, and business impact objectives for each program
- focusing the content of the program on performance improvement
- ensuring that exercises, tests, case studies, and skill practices relate to the desired objectives
- keeping participants focused on program objectives
- communicating rationale and reasons for evaluation
- assisting in follow-up activities to capture the appropriate data
- providing assistance for data collection, data analysis, and reporting

- developing plans for data collection and analysis
- presenting evaluation data to a variety of groups
- assisting with the design of instruments.

Although it may not be appropriate to have each staff member involved in all of these activities, each member should have at least one responsibility as part of his or her routine job duties. Assignment of responsibility keeps evaluation from becoming disconnected from major learning and development activities. More important, it brings accountability to those who develop, deliver, and implement programs.

The second group to which measurement and evaluation responsibilities should be assigned is the technical support function. Depending on the size of the learning and development staff, it may be helpful to establish a group of technical experts to provide assistance with measurement and evaluation. When this group is established, it must be clear that the experts are not there to relieve others of evaluation responsibilities, but to supplement technical expertise. Some organizations have found this approach to be effective. Accenture's measurement and evaluation staff provided technical support for the evaluation of internal professional education. When this type of support is developed, responsibilities revolve around several key areas:

- designing data collection instruments
- providing assistance for developing an evaluation strategy
- coordinating a major evaluation project
- analyzing data, including specialized statistical analyses
- interpreting results and making specific recommendations
- developing an evaluation report or case study to communicate overall results
- presenting results to critical audiences
- providing technical support in any phase of evaluation.

The assignment of responsibilities for evaluation to others is also an issue that needs attention throughout implementation. Although the learning and development staff must have specific responsibilities, it is not unusual to require others in support functions to have responsibility for data collection, analysis, interpretation, and review, as well.

Assess the Climate

Some organizations assess the current climate for achieving results with learning and development. Annual assessments are taken to measure progress as the measurement and evaluation process is implemented. Others assess the management group to determine the extent managers perceive learning and development to be effective. The use of an assessment process provides an understanding of current status. Then the organization can plan for changes and pinpoint particular issues that need support as the measurement and evaluation process is implemented. Appendix A presents an assessment instrument to assess the climate for measurement and evaluation for learning and development.

Establish Evaluation Targets

Specific targets for evaluation measures and projects are necessary to make progress with measurement and evaluation. Targets enable the learning and development staff to focus on the improvements needed within specific evaluation categories.

When establishing targets, the percentage of courses or programs planned for evaluation is determined. A case in point is establishing targets for evaluating programs at each of the five levels (Phillips & Phillips, 1999). The first step is to assess the present situation as shown in table 8-1. The number of all courses (or programs), including repeated sections of a course, is tabulated along with the corresponding level(s) of evaluation presently conducted for each program. Next, the percentage of programs using reaction data for evaluation is calculated. The process is repeated for learning, application, impact, and ROI evaluations.

After detailing the current situation, the next step is to determine a realistic target for each level within a specific timeframe. Many organizations set annual targets for changes. This process should involve the input of the learning and development staff to ensure that the targets are realistic and that the staff is committed to the evaluation process and targets. If the learning and development staff does not develop ownership for this process, targets will not be met. The improvement targets must be achievable, while at the same time, challenging and motivating.

Wachovia Bank, for example, evaluates 100 percent of its hundreds of programs with reaction data (level 1), which is consistent with many other organizations (J.J. Phillips, 2003). Only half of the programs are measured at level 2, using a formal method of learning measurement. At this organization, informal methods are not counted as a learning measure. The level 2 measure may increase significantly in groups where there is much formal testing, or if informal measures (for example, self-assessment) are included as a learning measure. Thirty percent of programs are measured at level 3 (application and implementation). This means that almost a third of the programs have some type of follow-up method implemented—at least for a small sample of participants in those programs. Ten percent of the programs are planned for business impact evaluation (level 4) and half of those for ROI (level 5). These

Table 8-1. Establishing evaluation targets.

	Number of Programs Offered	
	Current Situation	Target
1. Percentage of programs using reaction data:		
2. Percentage of programs using learning data:		
3. Percentage of programs using behavior change or application data:		
4. Percentage of programs using impact or business results data:		
5. Percentage of programs using ROI data:		

percentages are typical and often recommended. There is rarely a need to go beyond 10 and 5 percent for levels 4 and 5, respectively. Sometimes targets are established for gradual improvement of increasing evaluation process over several years.

Target setting is a critical implementation issue. It should be completed early in the implementation process with the full support of the entire learning and development staff. Also, when practical and feasible, the targets should have the approval of the key management staff, particularly the senior management team.

Develop a Project Plan for Implementation

An important part of the implementation process is to establish timetables for completion. The project plan becomes a master plan for overcoming resistance to implementation. The plan begins with assigning responsibilities and concludes with meeting the targets previously described. Figure 8-2 shows an implementation project plan for a large petroleum company.

From a practical basis, this project plan helps the learning and development staff make the transition from the present situation to a desired future situation. The items on the schedule include developing specific evaluation projects, building staff skills, developing policy, teaching managers the process, analyzing data, and communicating results. The more detailed the document, the more useful it becomes. The project plan is a living, long-range document that should be reviewed frequently and adjusted as necessary. More important, those routinely working with evaluation should be familiar with the plan and stay current with the progress.

Revise/Develop Policies and Procedures

Another key step in overcoming resistance to evaluation is revising (or developing) the organization's policy concerning measurement and evaluation. Research shows that those organizations with a formal evaluation policy tend to take a comprehensive approach to evaluation (P.P. Phillips, 2003). Developing evaluation policies frequently involves the input of the learning and development staff, key managers or sponsors, and the finance and accounting staff. Sometimes policy issues are addressed during internal workshops designed to build skills with measurement and evaluation. Figure 8-3 shows the topics in the measurement and evaluation policy for a large firm in South Africa.

Policy statements address critical issues that influence the effectiveness of the measurement and evaluation process. Policy statements are important because they provide guidance and direction for the staff and others who work with the evaluation process. They keep the process on track and enable the group to establish goals for evaluation. Policy statements also provide an opportunity to communicate basic requirements and fundamental issues

Figure 8-2. Implementation project plan for a large petroleum company.

	J	F	M	A	M	J	J	A	S	O	N	D	J	F	M	A	M	J	J	A	S	O	N
Team Formed	█																						
Policy Developed		█																					
Targets Set			█																				
Network Formed				█																			
Workshops Developed					█	█																	
Evaluation Project (A)							█	█															
Evaluation Project (B)								█	█	█													
Evaluation Project (C)										█	█												
Evaluation Project (D)												█	█	█									
Learning and Development Staff Trained													█										
Suppliers Trained														█									
Managers Trained															█	█							
Support Tools Developed				█																			
Evaluation Guidelines Developed				█	█																		

Source: Phillips, J.J. (2003). *Return on Investment in Training and Performance Improvement Programs.* Boston: Butterworth-Heinemann. Reprinted with permission.

Figure 8-3. Results-based internal learning and development policy (excerpts from actual policy for a large firm in South Africa).

1. Purpose
2. Mission
3. Evaluate all programs which will include the following levels:
   a. Participant satisfaction (100%)
   b. Learning (no less than 70%)
   c. Job applications (50%)
   d. Results (usually through sampling) (10%) (highly visible, expensive)
   e. ROI (5%)
4. Evaluation support group (corporate) will provide assistance and advice in Measurement & Evaluation, Instrument Design, Data Analysis, and Evaluation Strategy.
5. New programs are developed following logical steps beginning with needs analysis and ending with communicating results.
6. Evaluation instruments must be designed or selected to collect data for evaluation. They must be valid, reliable, economical, and subject to audit by evaluation support group.
7. Responsibility for learning and development program results rests with trainers, participants, and supervisors of participants.
8. An adequate system for collecting and monitoring learning and development costs must be in place. All direct costs should be included.
9. At least annually the management board will review the status and results of learning and development. The review will include learning and development plans, strategies, results, costs, priorities, and concerns.
10. Line management shares in the responsibility for learning and development programs. Evaluation through follow-up, pre-program commitments, and overall support.
11. Managers/supervisors must declare competence achieved through training and packaged programs. When not applicable, learning and development staff should evaluate.
12. External learning and development consultants must be selected based on previous evaluation. Central data/resource base should exist. All external learning and development programs of over one day in duration will be subjected to evaluation procedures. In addition, participants will assess the quality of external programs.
13. Learning and development program results must be communicated to the appropriate target audience. As a minimum, this includes management (participants' supervisor), participants, and all learning and development staff.
14. Learning and development staff should be qualified to do effective needs analysis and evaluation.
15. Central database for program development to prevent duplication and serve as program resource.
16. Union involvement in total learning and development plan.

Source: Phillips, J.J. (1997). *Handbook of Training and Evaluation and Measurement Methods,* 3rd edition. Boston: Butterworth-Heinemann. Reprinted with permission.

regarding performance and accountability. More than anything else, they serve as a learning tool to teach others, especially when they are developed in a collaborative way. If policy statements are developed in isolation and exclude the ownership of the staff and management, they will not be effective or useful.

Guidelines for measurement and evaluation are important to show how to use the tools and techniques, guide the design process, provide consis-tency with evaluation, ensure that appropriate methods are used, and place the proper emphasis on each of the areas. The guidelines are more technical than they are policy statements. Evaluation guidelines often contain detailed procedures showing how evaluation is actually undertaken and developed. They may include specific forms, instruments, and tools necessary to facilitate the process. Figure 8-4 shows the table of contents for evaluation guidelines for a multinational company.

Involve the Learning and Development Staff

One group that often resists implementing a comprehensive measurement and evaluation process is the learning and development staff, who must design, develop, deliver, and coordinate training and learning solutions. These staff members often see evaluation as an unnecessary intrusion into their responsibilities, absorbing precious time and stifling their freedom to be creative.

The learning and development staff should be involved in each key issue and decision. As policy statements are prepared and evaluation guidelines developed, staff input is absolutely essential. It is difficult for the staff to be critical of something they helped design, develop, plan, and implement. Using workshops, brainstorming sessions, planning sessions, and taskforces, the staff should be involved in every phase of developing the framework and supporting documents.

The learning and development staff members may sometimes resist measurement and evaluation because their programs are then fully exposed, placing their reputation on the line. They may have a fear of failure. Learning and development staff members will not be interested in developing a tool that will be used to expose their shortcomings and failures. To overcome this, the measurement and evaluation process should be positioned clearly as a tool for process improvement and not a tool to evaluate learning and development staff performance, at least during its early years of implementation.

Evaluators can often learn more from failures than from successes. If the program is not working, it is best to find out quickly and understand the issues firsthand—not from others. If a program is ineffective and not producing the desired results, it will eventually be known to clients and the management group, if they are not aware of it already. A lack of results can cause managers to become less supportive of learning and development. Dwindling support appears in many forms, ranging from budget reductions to refusals to allow employees to participate in programs. When the weaknesses of programs are identified and adjustments are made quickly, ineffective programs are converted to effective programs, and the credibility and respect for the learning and development function and staff is enhanced.

Teach the Staff

The learning and development staff usually lack specialized skills in measurement and evaluation; therefore, most need to develop expertise in the process. Measurement and evaluation is not always a formal part of preparing to become a facilitator, instructional designer, or performance analyst. Consequently, each staff member needs training to learn how evaluation is implemented, step by step. In addition, staff members must know how to develop plans to collect and analyze data and interpret results from data analysis. A one- or two-day workshop can help build adequate skills and knowledge to understand the process, appreciate what it can accomplish for the organization, see the necessity for it, and participate in a successful implementation. Each staff member should know how to understand, utilize, and support evaluation.

Select Programs for Impact Evaluation

Selecting a program for a major evaluation study is an important issue. Ideally, certain types of programs should be selected for comprehensive, detailed analyses. The typical approach for identifying programs for evaluation is to select those that are expensive, strategic, and highly visible. Figure 8-5 lists six of the common criteria often used to select programs for this level of evaluation.

These are only the basic criteria; you can extend the list as necessary to bring the organization's particular issues into focus. Some large organizations with hundreds of programs use as many as 15 criteria. The learning and development staff rates programs based on these criteria, using a rating scale of 1–5. All programs are rated and the program with the highest number is the best candidate for impact evaluation consideration. This process

Figure 8-4. Evaluation guidelines for a multinational company.

Section 1: Policy
1.1 The Need for Accountability
1.2 The Bottom Line: Linking Training with Business Needs
1.3 Results-Based Approach
1.4 Implications
1.5 Communication
1.6 Payoff

Section 2: Responsibilities
2.1 Training Group Responsibilities: Overall
2.2 Training Group Responsibilities: Specifics for Selected Groups
2.3 The Business Unit Responsibilities
2.4 Participant Manager Responsibilities
2.5 Participant Responsibilities

Section 3: Evaluation Framework
3.1 Purpose of Evaluation
3.2 Levels of Evaluation
3.3 Process Steps for Training Implementation
3.4 Evaluation Model

Section 4: Level 1 Guidelines
4.1 Purpose and Scope
4.2 Areas of Coverage—Standard Form
4.3 Optional Areas of Coverage
4.4 Administrative Issues
4.5 How to Use Level 1 Data

Section 5: Level 2 Guidelines
5.1 Purpose and Scope
5.2 Learning Measurement Issues
5.3 Techniques for Measuring Learning
5.4 Administration
5.5 Using Level 2 Data

Section 6: Level 3 Guidelines
6.1 Purpose and Scope
6.2 Follow-Up Issues
6.3 Types of Follow-Up Techniques
6.4 Administrative Issues
6.5 Using Level 3 Evaluation

Section 7: Level 4 and 5 Guidelines
7.1 Purpose and Scope
7.2 Business Results and ROI Issues
7.3 Monitoring Performance Data
7.4 Extracting Data from Follow-Up Evaluation
7.5 Isolating the Effects of the Learning Solution
7.6 Converting Data to Monetary Values
7.7 Developing Costs
7.8 Calculating ROI
7.9 Identifying Intangible Benefits
7.10 Administrative Issues
7.11 Using Business Impact and ROI Data

Figure 8-5. Tool for selecting studies for impact studies.

Programs

Criterion	#1	#2	#3	#4	#5
1. Life Cycle					
2. Company Objectives					
3. Costs					
4. Audience Size					
5. Visibility					
6. Management Interest					
Total					

Rating Scale

1. Life Cycle	5 = Long lifecycle 1 = Very short lifecycle
2. Company Objectives	5 = Closely related to company objectives 1 = Not directly related to company objectives
3. Costs	5 = Very expensive 1 = Very inexpensive
4. Audience Size	5 = Very large audience 1 = Very small audience
5. Visibility	5 = High visibility 1 = Low visibility
6. Management Interest	5 = High level of interest in evaluation 1 = Low level of interest in evaluation

Source: Phillips, P.P., and H. Burkett. (2001). "Managing Evaluation Shortcuts." *Infoline*, no. 25011. Alexandria, VA: ASTD. Reprinted with permission.

only identifies the best candidates. The actual number evaluated may depend on other factors, resources, and capability.

The most important aspect is to select programs that are designed to make a difference and represent significant investments. Also, programs that command much attention from management are ideal candidates for a major evaluation. Almost any senior management group has an idea about the effectiveness of a particular program. Some want to know its impact, whereas others are not all that concerned. For these reasons, management interest often drives the selection of many evaluation studies.

The next step is to determine how many impact evaluation projects to undertake initially and in which particular areas. It's a good idea to start small by taking perhaps two or three programs to impact-level evaluation. It is important to select a manageable number so the process will be implemented when considering the constraints. The selected programs may represent the functional areas of the business such as operations, sales, finance, engineering, or information systems. Another approach is to select programs representing functional areas of learning and development such as sales training, executive and management development, team leader development, computer-based training, or technical training.

You should consider a few additional criteria when selecting initial programs for impact evaluation.

For example, the initial program should be as simple as possible. Complex programs should be reserved until skills have been mastered. Also, the initial program should be one that is considered successful now; that is, all the current feedback data suggests that the program is adding significant value. This way, you can probably avoid having a negative impact study on the first use of the impact analysis. Still another criterion is to select a program that is devoid of strong political issues or biases. Although these programs can be tackled effectively with impact analysis, it may be too much of a challenge for an early application.

Ultimately, the number of programs tackled depends on the resources available to conduct the studies as well as the internal need for accountability. But even the rigorous system of program evaluation undertaken by Wachovia Bank, outlined previously in this chapter, requires only about 3 to 5 percent of the organization's total learning and development budget. The costs of evaluation do not necessarily drain the resources of the organization.

Report Progress on Studies

As evaluation projects are developed and the implementation is under way, status meetings should be conducted to report progress and discuss critical issues with appropriate team members. For example, if a leadership program is selected as one of the projects, all of the key staff involved in the program (design, development, and delivery) should meet regularly to discuss the status of the project. This approach keeps the project team focused on the critical issues, generates the best ideas to tackle particular problems and barriers, and builds a knowledge base to implement evaluation in future programs. Sometimes this group is facilitated by an external consultant, an expert in evaluation. In other cases, the internal evaluation leader may facilitate the group.

These meetings serve three major purposes: reporting progress, learning, and planning. The meeting usually begins with a status report on each project to describe what's been accomplished since the previous meeting. Next, the specific barriers and problems encountered are discussed. During the discussions, new issues are interjected for possible tactics, techniques, or tools. Also, the entire group discusses how to remove barriers to success and focuses on suggestions and recommendations for next steps, including developing specific plans. Finally, the next steps are developed, discussed, and configured.

Prepare the Management Team

Perhaps no group is more important to the measurement and evaluation process than the management team who must allocate resources for learning and development and who must support the programs. In addition, the team often provides input and assistance for the evaluation process. Specific actions to train and develop the management team should be carefully planned and executed. Also, the relationship between the learning and development staff and key managers must be improved. A productive partnership requires each party to understand the concerns, problems, and opportunities of the other. Developing this type of relationship is a long-term process that requires deliberate planning and initiation by key learning and development staff members. Sometimes the decision to commit resources and support for learning solutions is often based on the effectiveness of this relationship.

Remove Barriers to Implementation

Several barriers to the implementation of evaluation exist. Some of these are realistic barriers, while others are often based on misconceptions. Here are a few barriers that you're likely to encounter, involving the learning and development staff:

- *Evaluation is a complex process.* The learning and development staff will perceive evaluation as too complex to implement. To counter this perception, the staff must understand that by breaking the process down into individual components and steps, it can be simplified. Tools, templates, and software are available to simplify evaluation. The resources listed at various places in this book contain many of these tools.

- *Learning and development staff members don't have time for evaluation.* Although evaluation does take additional time, the learning and development staff need to understand that evaluation can save time in the long run. An evaluation report may show that the program should be changed, modified, or even eliminated. Also, up-front planning with evaluation strategy can save additional follow-up time. Sometimes it is a matter of priority.

- *The learning and developing staff must be motivated to pursue evaluations, even when senior executives are not requiring it.* Most staff members know when top managers are pushing the accountability issue. If they do not see that push, learning and development staff are reluctant to take the time to make it work. They must see the benefits of pursuing the process even if it is not required by the top. The staff should see evaluation as a preventive strategy or a leading-edge strategy. The payoff of evaluation should be underscored.

- *The learning and development staff may be concerned that results will lead to criticism.* Many staff members might be concerned about the use of evaluation data. If the results are used to criticize or reflect on the performance of program designers or facilitators, they will be reluctant to embrace the concept. Evaluation should be considered as process improvement. The learning and development leader must manage this issue throughout implementation of measurement and evaluation.

These and other obstacles can thwart an otherwise successful implementation. Each must be removed or reduced to a manageable issue.

Making Evaluation Routine

For lasting value, measurement and evaluation must be perceived as routine, not a one-time event or an add-on process. It must be considered early and often in the learning and development cycle. Evaluation studies must be planned and integrated into the learning and development as early as possible. The tasks, processes, and procedures of evaluation must be as painless as possible, increasing the odds that they will be used routinely. When evaluation becomes routine, it will become an accepted and important—and sometimes required—element in the learning and development cycle.

Make Planning Routine

Intuitively, most professionals realize that planning is an important way to minimize problems, reduce resources, and stay focused on the outcome. Nowhere is this more true than when planning a comprehensive evaluation. Planning minimizes the time required later, keeps the evaluation efficient and less expensive, and helps all stakeholders to become focused on tasks and processes. It also serves to gain buy-in from key clients. More important, it helps make evaluation routine. Planning is essential whenever a major evaluation study is conducted. Even if the program has been operational for some time and the evaluation is suddenly requested, planning is needed to decide how to collect, process, and report data. Ideally, the evaluation plan should be in place before the program is actually developed so that the planning may actually influence the design, development, and delivery of the learning and development program.

Planning involves three phases, each generating its own unique document. The first phase is data collection. Figure 8-6 shows a completed data collection plan for a four-day leadership development program. This document organizes the collection of data around the different levels of evaluation, beginning with the objectives arranged by level and depicts what was expected at that level. Next, specific measures are defined. If details contained in the objective itself are insufficient, clarification is needed. For example, if a learning program was designed to improve productivity (an impact measure), more detail is needed to define how the organization actually measures productivity. Next, the data collection method, whether interview, questionnaire, focus group, observation, or records monitoring, is detailed. The source of the data is included along with the timing of the data collection. Finally the responsibilities for data collection are delineated.

A data analysis plan defines in more detail how the data will be processed after it is collected. Figure 8-7 shows a typical data analysis form. The beginning point in the plan is the business impact data that will be influenced by the program. The specific method of isolating the effects of the program on those data is identified. Next, the method of converting data to monetary value is indicated, if monetary impact is actually pursued in the evaluation. In many situations, clients want to see the actual monetary value; and, of course, if the evaluation is taken to the ROI level, the monetary value must be developed. The cost of the program being evaluated is determined, including all direct and indirect costs. For planning purposes, cost categories will suffice. A detailed cost summary is developed later. Next, the anticipated intangibles are included. Intangible items are those measures not converted to monetary value but linked to the program. They represent very important data. Finally, the target groups for communicating the results of the evaluation are included with any other comments and issues that might influence the evaluation. This document is important when detail analysis is planned particularly with business impact and ROI.

The final step is the communication and implementation plan for the evaluation study. This plan details the sequence of events as they should occur from the time that the evaluation plan is developed until all information has been communicated. Communication audiences, media, and timing are identified. Responsibility for actions is indicated.

These planning documents can be completed in a matter of hours when the various team members and stakeholders are available to provide input. The payoff is tremendous, as planning not only makes the process more efficient and faster but it enhances the likelihood that it will become routine.

Integrate Evaluation Into Learning and Development Programs

One of the most effective ways to make evaluation routine is to build it into the program. This approach changes the perception of evaluation from an add-on process to one that is an integral part of the application of learning.

Built-in evaluation can be accomplished in several ways. One of the most effective is to use action plans that serve as application tools for the skills and knowledge learned in the program. The action plan is included as part of the program, and its requirement is communicated early. Appropriate agenda time is taken to explain how to develop and use the action plan. Sometimes participants are provided time to complete it. The follow-up on success of the action plan provides data for evaluation. In this context, the action plan becomes an application tool instead of an evaluation tool. The commitment to the participants is that the completed action plan data will be summarized for the entire sample group and returned to them so that each member can see what others have accomplished. This provides a little of "what's in it for me" for the participants. Today, action plans are being used to drive not only application and implementation data, but business impact data as well.

Another built-in technique is to enclose the follow-up questionnaire along with the learning and development program. Ample time should be given to review the items on the questionnaire and secure a commitment to provide data. This step-by-step review of expectations helps clarify confusing issues and improves response rates as participants make a commitment to provide the data. This easy to accomplish step can be a powerful way to enhance

Figure 8-6. Example of a completed data collection plan.

Data Collection Plan

Program: The Leadership Challenge **Responsibility:** **Date:**

Level	Objective(s)	Measures/Data	Data Collection Method	Data Sources	Timing	Responsibilities
1	**Reaction/Satisfaction** • Participants rate the program as relevant to their jobs • Participants rate the program as important to their job success	• Rating of 4 on a 5-point rating scale	• Questionnaire	• Participants	• End of Program	• Facilitator
2	**Learning** • Participants demonstrate acceptable performance on each major competency	• Rating of 2 on a 3-point scale	• Observation of skill practices • Self-assessment via questionnaire	• Facilitator • Participants	• End of Program • End of Program	• Facilitator • Facilitator
3	**Application/Implementation** • Participants utilize the competencies with team members on a routine basis	• Various measures (ratings, open-ended items, etc.)	• Questionnaire • Questionnaire	• Participants • Participants' Manager	• 3 months	• Learning and Development Staff
4	**Business Impact** • Participants and team members drive improvements in at least two business measures	• Various work unit measures	• Questionnaire	• Participants	• 3 months	• Learning and Development Staff
5	**ROI** • Achieve a 20% ROI					

Comments:

Source: Phillips, J.J., and L. Schmidt. (2004). *The Leadership Scorecard.* Boston: Butterworth-Heinemann. Reprinted with permission.

Figure 8-7. Example of a completed data analysis plan.

Data Analysis Plan

Program: ___ The Leadership Challenge ___ Responsibility: ___ Date: ___

Data Items (Usually Level 4)	Methods for Isolating the Effects of the Program/ Process	Methods of Converting Data to Monetary Values	Cost Categories	Intangible Benefits	Communication Targets for Final Report	Other Influences/ Issues During Application	Comments
• Varies, depending on measures selected	• Participant estimate	• Standard value • Expert value • Participant estimate	• Needs assess-ment (prorated) • Program develop-ment (prorated) • Facilitation fees • Promotional materials • Facilitation and coordination • Meals and refreshments • Facilities • Participant salaries and benefits for time away from work • Managers' salaries and benefits for time involved in program • Overhead • Evaluation	• Job satisfaction for first-level managers • Job satisfaction for team members • Improved teamwork • Improved communication	• Participants (first-level managers) • Participants' managers • Senior executives • Learning and development staff • Prospective participants • Learning and development council members	• Several process improvement initiatives are on-going during this program implementation	• Must gain commitment to provide data • A high response rate is needed

Source: Phillips, J.J., and L. Schmidt. (2004). *The Leadership Scorecard*. Boston: Butterworth-Heinemann. Reprinted with permission.

data collection. It prevents constant reminders for participants to provide data at a later follow-up.

Reaction and learning evaluation are almost always built into the learning and development program as reaction and learning measures are routinely captured. Still, application and impact data can be collected during the successive learning programs as well. For example, in one organization, participants attended a series of modules. Follow-up data on the application of previous modules was always captured in the next module. In essence, a collection of data was built into the learning process as it became routine. Those and other ways help to build evaluation into the learning design and create a powerful way to make evaluation routine by reducing the amount of time needed to collect data and sharing the responsibilities with others. This leads to the next item.

Use Shortcuts

One of the most significant barriers to the implementation of measurement and evaluation is the potential time and cost involved in implementing the process. An important tradeoff exists between the task of additional analysis versus the use of shortcut methods, including estimation. In those tradeoffs, shortcuts win almost every time. An increasing amount of research shows shortcuts and estimations, when provided by those who know a process best (experts), can be even more accurate than more sophisticated, detailed analysis (Sutcliffe & Weber, 2001). Essentially, evaluators try to avoid the high costs of increasing accuracy because it just doesn't pay off.

Sometimes, the perception of excessive time and cost is only a myth; at other times it is a reality. As discussed earlier, most organizations can implement the evaluation methodology for about 3 to 5 percent of the learning and development budget. Nevertheless, evaluation still commands significant time and monetary resources. The following cost-saving approaches have commanded much attention recently and represent an important part of the implementation strategy (Phillips & Burkett, 2001).

Take Shortcuts at Lower Levels. When resources are a primary concern and shortcuts need to be taken, it is best to take them at lower levels in the evaluation scheme. This is a resource allocation issue. For example, if an impact evaluation (level 4) is conducted, levels 1–3 do not have to be as comprehensive. This shift places most of the emphasis on the highest level of the evaluation.

Fund Measurement and Evaluation With Program Cost Saving. Almost every impact study generates data from which to make improvements. Results at different levels often show how the program can be altered to make it more effective and efficient. Sometimes, the data suggests that the program can be modified, adjusted, or completely redesigned. Any of those actions can lead to cost savings. In a few cases, the program may have to be eliminated because it is not adding value and adjustments will not result in an improved program. In this case, substantial cost savings can be realized as the program is eliminated. A logical argument can be made to shift a portion of these savings to fund additional measurement and evaluation. Some organizations gradually migrate to the 5 percent of budget target for expenditures for measurement and evaluation by utilizing the savings generated from the use of evaluation. This provides a disciplined and conservative approach to additional funding.

Use Participants. One of the most effective cost-saving approaches is to have participants conduct major steps of the process. Participants are the primary source for understanding the degree to which learning is applied and has driven success on the job. The responsibilities for the participants should be expanded from the traditional requirement of involvement in learning activities and application of new skills. They must be asked to show the impact of those new skills and provide data about success as a routine part of the process. Consequently, the role of the participant has expanded from learning and application to measuring the impact and communicating information.

Use Quick Methods. For many evaluation processes, quick, but credible, shortcut methods are available. For example, in data collection, the simple questionnaire is a shortcut method that can be used to generate powerful and convincing data, if administered properly. This inexpensive data collection method can be used in many evaluations. Other shortcut methods are available when isolating the effects of learning and converting data to monetary values.

Use Sampling. Not all programs require comprehensive evaluation, nor should all participants necessarily be evaluated in a planned follow-up. Thus, sampling can be used in two ways. First, as described earlier, you may select only a few programs for impact evaluation. Those programs should be selected based on the criteria described earlier in this book. Next, when a particular program is evaluated, in most cases, only a sample of participants should be evaluated to keep costs and time to a minimum.

Use Estimates. Estimates are an important part of the process. They are also the least expensive way to arrive at a number or value. Whether isolating the effects of learning or converting data to monetary value, estimates can be a routine and credible part of the process. In these scenarios, the participants are actually the experts because they understand their own performance better than anyone else. They understand the impact they had and the various factors that have influenced the impact. The important point is to make sure the estimate is credible and follows systematic, logical, consistent steps.

Use Internal Resources. An organization does not necessarily have to employee consultants to develop impact studies and address other measurement and evaluation issues. Internal capability can be developed, eliminating the need to depend on consultants. Several opportunities to build skills and become certified in evaluation are available and were presented in chapter 5. This approach is perhaps one of the most significant time savers. The difference in using internal resources versus external consultants can save as much as 50 or 60 percent of the costs of a specific project.

Build on the Work of Others. No one has time to reinvent the wheel. One of the most important cost-saving approaches is to learn from others and build on their work. Capitalize on networking opportunities internally, locally, and globally, as described in chapter 5. You can also learn a great deal by reading and dissecting published case studies. More than 100 cases have been published, some of which are listed in the Additional Resources section of this book.

Use Standard Templates. Most organizations don't have the time and resources to customize each evaluation project. To the extent possible, develop standard instruments that can be used over and over. If customization is needed, it is only a minor part of it.

For example, the reaction questionnaire should be standardized and automated to save time and to make evaluation routine. Learning measurements can be standard and built into the reaction evaluation questionnaire, unless more objective methods are needed, such as testing, simulation, and skill practices. Follow-up evaluation questionnaires (for application and impact) can be standard, with only a part of the questionnaire to be customized, if necessary. Patterned interviews can be developed as standard processes. Focus group agendas also can be standard. The important point is to standardize as much as possible so that evaluation forms are not reinvented for each application. As a result, tabulation is faster and often less expense. When this is accomplished, evaluation will be routine (Phillips & Burkett, in press).

Build Skills With the Staff. When learning and development staff members understand how to conduct evaluation studies, resistance diminishes. It is natural for individuals to avoid processes they do not understand. The more the staff understands about the evaluation process and how to perform the different steps and tasks, the more they will make it a routine part of what they do. To make evaluation routine, the staff members must understand not only the purpose, scope, and intent of evaluation in the organization, but also how to make it work with minimum resources. This degree of efficiency requires building competency and capability.

Streamline Reporting. Reporting data can be one of the most time-consuming parts of evaluation, taking precious time away from data collection, processing, and analysis. Yet, reporting is often the most critical part of the process, as many audiences need a variety of information. Two key components are involved:

- the actual report or content that is presented to the various audiences
- the method of disseminating the information.

Both components can take too much time. The bad news is that a comprehensive evaluation process generates significant data to be summarized and distributed to a variety of target audiences. The good news is that reporting can take a variety of formats suited to the audience's needs, with some of this being very brief. When the audience understands the evaluation methodology, they can usually digest information in a brief format. For example, it is possible to present the results of an impact study using a one-page format, as described in chapter 6. It is, however, essential for the audience to understand fully the approach to evaluation and the principles and assumptions behind the methodology; otherwise, they will not understand what the data actually means. Face-to-face meetings are used within the group initially, with one of the goals of the meeting to help them understand the evaluation methodology. Afterwards, shortcut methods can be used. Figure 8-8 shows the progression of reporting major impact studies in one organization.

Reporting can also be streamlined as you develop the complete evaluation study. With similar studies, a template can be developed with minor changes. For example, in one organization where a performance management program was conducted for new store managers, a template was developed to report the results to the executive group. This 50-page template on the success of the program only took about four hours to complete. Although the program was offered 10 times per year, a report was generated after each follow-up evaluation to satisfy a variety of audience needs. It was not so time consuming because the template was already generated. In some cases, software is available to help develop reporting much faster and on a standard basis. This leads to the final strategy that can help make evaluation routine.

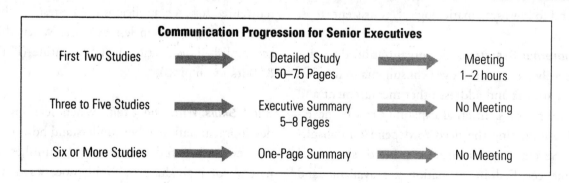

Figure 8-8. Streamlining communication with executives.

Communication Progression for Senior Executives

First Two Studies	→	Detailed Study 50–75 Pages	→	Meeting 1–2 hours
Three to Five Studies	→	Executive Summary 5–8 Pages	→	No Meeting
Six or More Studies	→	One-Page Summary	→	No Meeting

Use Technology. A plethora of software tools is available to help organizations develop consistent processes, use standard techniques, and generate consistent reports. Technology is absolutely essential when collecting reaction and learning data from many different programs. Software not only reduces the time for data collection, but also the time necessary to develop and report information, often in the form of a scorecard or a report generated by the software. Although several software packages are available, one recommended software is from KnowledgeAdvisors (www.knowledgeadvisors.com). This software develops reaction, learning, application, impact, and ROI data and also generates scorecards and reports. Chapter 5, on expertise and resources, contains more detail on technology requirements.

All the shortcuts described in this chapter are important to ensure that evaluation does not unnecessarily drain budgets and resources. Other shortcuts can be developed, but a word of caution is in order: Shortcuts often compromise the process. When a comprehensive, valid, and reliable study is needed, it will be time consuming and expensive—there's no way around it.

The good news is that many shortcuts can be taken to supply the data necessary for the audience and manage the process in an efficient way. All these shortcuts are important processes that can help make evaluation routine because when evalua-tion is expensive, time consuming, and difficult, it will never become routine.

Final Thoughts

In summary, the key to overcoming resistance to evaluation is developing a step-by-step implementation strategy. Carefully putting in place the building blocks identified in this chapter can help soothe fears and remove barriers, ensuring opportunity to successfully integrate and—more important—sustain a comprehensive measurement and evaluation process.

This chapter presented the different elements that must be considered and issues that must be addressed to overcome evaluation resistance. After describing these issues, a variety of strategies were outlined that can be implemented to minimize, reduce, or sometimes even remove a particular fear. These are the key issues that are often involved in implementation of measurement and evaluation.

Next, you learned about the actions needed to make evaluation routine. Although it is important to get evaluation started and implemented in the organization, it must become routine to add significant value over time. When evaluation becomes routine, it will become an integral part of the organization and be sustained over a long-term period. The chapter explored a full array of possibilities to bring routine to the evaluation process, while reducing the resources required for implementation.

9

Evaluation Ethics and Standards

● ●

This final chapter describes some of the most important issues facing evaluators: ethics and standards. Ethical issues can destroy the results of evaluation, erode the credibility of the evaluator, and undermine the trust and confidence of stakeholders. Worse still, unethical practices can be harmful to individuals involved in evaluation studies. Several ethical traps await the evaluator. This chapter explores these ethical traps and issues. You can avoid these traps with proper planning and ethical behavior.

Finally, standards are needed for evaluation not only for ethical issues but also for consistency and reliability of the evaluation process as well. Although additional details on standards are needed, this chapter provides information on the available standards.

● ●

Practicing acceptable ethics is critical to the success of an evaluation project. Ethics involves the behavior of the evaluator, the rules followed throughout the process, communications with stakeholders, the expectations created with participants, and the relationships developed throughout the project. Stakeholders must understand the role of ethics and their role in ethical behavior. Acceptable ethics represent a desired way of operating that should not create conflicts for the client. Most clients want an ethical project, and client satisfaction can be achieved with ethical behavior.

The goal of this chapter is to ensure that the evaluator is aware of ethical problems looming in their potential projects. It also prescribes steps to avoid them. This approach does not suggest that being ethical is just a matter of doing the right thing; rather it is a matter of adopting ethical behavior, using integrity, establishing trust, and being fair and honest throughout the evaluation.

Ethical Problems

Ethical issues may frequently appear throughout a project. They can sometimes derail the entire project and destroy the relationships between the evaluator and the clients. Sometimes a lack of ethics results in formal complaints or litigation. Serious ethical dilemmas faced by evaluators can be prevented or avoided by following strict guidelines and openly communicating expectations, roles, and responsibilities.

A study conducted by Newman and Brown (1992) asked a sample of 145 respondents to list the most important ethical violations of 30 evaluation standards. Respondents thought the following five were most serious violations:

- The evaluator changes the evaluation questions to match the data analysis.
- The evaluator promises confidentiality when it cannot be guaranteed.
- The evaluator makes decisions without consulting with the client when consultation has been agreed to.

- The evaluator conducts an evaluation when he or she lacks sufficient skills or experience.
- Evaluation reports are written in such a way that partisan interest groups can delete embarrassing weaknesses.

The problems vary, as do the opportunities for danger. The key is to build the correct approach into the project from the beginning.

Preventing Ethical Issues

The rest of this chapter focuses on some prescriptive processes to help focus on this critical issue.

Evaluator's Personal Ethics

The first area for consideration is the personal conduct of the evaluator—issues the evaluator should address in every project. The following issues transcend ethical behavior and define good client relationships:

1. *Provide quality work.* Providing value-added work to the client is the key responsibility of the evaluator. If your work is accurate, timely, and consistent you can avoid ethical issues created by errors, omissions, inconsistencies, and other quality-related problems.

2. *Ensure qualifications for the project.* Evaluators must have the skills and expertise to conduct the evaluation study. Pretending to have skills or competencies that do not exist is a serious problem. Sometimes it is best to admit to the sponsor or client that the capability is not there, avoiding many problems associated with substandard work.

3. *Learn to say "no" or "I don't know."* Evaluators need to be honest with clients and let them know if they do not have the information needed if they are unsure. One of the most refreshing comments to the client is for the evaluator to admit that he or she does not have all the answers.

4. *Avoid conflicts of interest.* Conflicts of interest can surface if the evaluator has a particular interest, ownership, or connection to the project being evaluated. If there is a relationship to individuals involved in the project, a conflict of interest may exist. All of these situations can be avoided with an upfront assessment of this issue before beginning a project. If the conflict turns out to be a surprise, acknowledge it as quickly as possible and rectify it.

5. *Submit charges appropriately.* An important issue in any type of transaction, appropriate charging is a fundamental business requirement. Only the time used on the project should be charged. All expenses must be legitimate and related to the project.

6. *Adhere to proposals.* Problems can crop up when there are deviations with what was planned and what was delivered. The proposal often outlines the scope of the work and the plan for the project. It is important to follow through with the plan and not make adjustments unless the client asks for or approves the changes. Changes should be documented. This approach keeps a clear understanding of expectations and deliverables for the project.

7. *Under-promise and over-deliver.* Creating unrealistic expectations can cause tremendous problems with a project. The evaluator should not promise something that he or she cannot deliver. Avoid promising specific response rates, for example, or even predicting the outcome of the project. Also, while low expectations may be created in terms of how the project may unfold, every attempt should be made to over-deliver, capturing all of the data and presenting the results in the most effective way.

8. *Respect the confidentiality and anonymity of the data sources.* Much evaluation data is collected anonymously or with the understanding that the input will be treated with confidentiality. These two issues need to be defined and communicated to the participants and strictly followed.

Appropriate personal ethics should become a routine mode of operation as evaluators assist clients and sponsors with projects. These actions establish productive relationships and build trust.

Ken Blanchard says that his company's ethical policy is defined by three simple questions: First, they ask the question, "Is it legal?" Ken Blanchard Companies wants to make sure that everything it does is in compliance with pertinent regulations and laws, particularly as they relate to client billing. Second, "Is it fair for all parties?" The organization wants its efforts to be a win-win for the client and consultant. Third, "How would we feel if the issue were printed in the newspaper and made public? Is it something we would be proud of or embarrassed about?" According to Blanchard, these principles provide guidance in resolving what could be potential ethical dilemmas and issues (Blanchard, 2002).

Remaining Independent and Being Objective

One of the most important challenges for evaluators is to operate independently. This may be difficult for learning and development staff members for whom evaluation is a part-time responsibility and the remaining responsibility is connected to some part or all of a learning or development program that is being evaluated. Even so, there are some steps that can be taken to remain as independent as possible:

■ *Operate independently.* If feasible, operate independently of any particular program or project that is being evaluated. This approach is possible in larger organizations where the individual conducting the evaluation is independent of the design, development, delivery, coordination, and ownership of a targeted learning program.

This is the ideal opportunity and provides a natural situation to be independent. If this is not feasible, other approaches may be possible.

■ *Use external providers.* As discussed in earlier chapters, some organizations outsource evaluation, relying on external consultants to conduct evaluation studies. This is accomplished in some organizations at a reasonable cost. Data collection is usually automated, and external services provide analysis and reporting. For major projects, consultants are available to conduct complete evaluation studies and present the data while still remaining independent.

■ *Pick a partner.* In many organizations, the evaluation function is a part-time responsibility of several learning and development staff members and the opportunity to partner is available. In these cases, a staff member develops the evaluation plan with the data collection in place. The data is returned to a partner for initial tabulation and summary. The individual staff member volunteers the same role for the partner. In essence these two individuals exchange responsibility for data collection, summary, and initial analysis.

■ *Consider low-cost data collection providers.* In some cases, external providers are available to collect, summarize, and return data in a raw, summarized form. Consultants, professors, and graduate students are available to provide this service. This approach has the advantage of providing objective data collection and tabulation, preventing data from being omitted, changed, or enhanced. In this situation, it is important to include all the raw data in the report so that the stakeholders can see what was provided.

■ *Acknowledge the issue and work with it.* In some situations, the evaluator must acknowledge a potential conflict of interest.

The audience must understand that the evaluator is involved or interested in parts or all of the program design, development, or delivery. The upfront acknowledgment helps build trust. Then, the evaluator can show all of the data that was returned. Ideally, the data is sent to an assistant who enters the data into the database; the appendix contains the raw data. Although this is not an optimal situation, it acknowledges to stakeholders—particularly those who fund learning and development programs—that there is some independence from the ownership, attempting to avoid a potential conflict of interest.

Typical Ethical Issues in Evaluation Projects

Several opportunities for unethical behavior surface when launching an evaluation project. A few possibilities are outlined in table 9-1.

Addressing Ethics During a Project

Several guidelines can help ensure that ethical issues are avoided during project implementation. The following operating guidelines keep the project focused and free of mistrust and errors:

1. *Communicate expectations.* Make sure that all stakeholders (especially the sponsors of the project) clearly understand what is expected from the project—the deliverables, the timing, and other important issues.

2. *Clarify roles.* Ensuring that every stakeholder involved knows his or her role in the project is critical. Unclear roles can lead to omissions or to unnecessary or excessive involvement on the part of a particular stakeholder.

3. *Show how results are used.* From an ethical perspective, it is important for individuals to understand how the data is to be used. Most evaluations lead to conclusions and,

Table 9-1. Potential ethical problems encountered during program evaluations.

Ethical Dilemma	Description	Possible Solution
Project Selection	Selecting programs to evaluate when multiple programs are possible may be a potential problem. The concern develops when an individual is involved in an evaluation where there is either conflict or the evaluator's capability does not exist.	Matching the evaluator with a project can help avoid an ethical dilemma. Also, ensuring that there is appropriate competence to conduct the evaluation is an important consideration.
Team Participation	Purposely omitting certain groups or individuals can generate ethical issues.	Deciding who will be on the evaluation team is important. Making sure that all stakeholders are represented and are involved in some way is essential. The extent to which others are actually involved in guiding or developing the outcome is important. While their input is essential, they should not be able to advise, alter, or change the outcomes in any way.
Data Collection	The greatest opportunity for unethical issues to arise is during data collection. Improper sampling; skewed questions on questionnaires, surveys, or for focus groups; and evaluator bias are all serious problems that can occur during data collection.	It is important to collect data from all the appropriate individuals, ensuring representation of the entire group. An appropriate degree of statistical rigor can help ensure that the data collected is representative and that evaluator bias is avoided.
Data Omission	One of the most disturbing ethical issues is the selective omission of data by those involved in data collection. This involves the overt action of purposely leaving data out of the analysis, destroying data, using selective follow-up in certain areas where data is desired, omitting specific types of comments.	An appropriate degree of statistical rigor can help ensure that the data collected is representative and that evaluator bias is avoided. All data should be made available for review.
Data Analysis, Interpretation, and Conclusions	Data interpretation can be subjective and even judgmental and should be approached with caution.	Including and itemizing all of the data are important. Selecting analytical techniques that are fair, consistent, and methodical is important. Using logical, rational approaches to reach conclusions is important, interpreting data in a way to minimize the possibility of bias, error, and misjudgment.
Identity Protection	Credibility can be destroyed if participants' responses can be tied to their identity.	Protecting the identity of all participants is very important even if it is not a condition for response. While it may be important to know the job group and some job characteristics of the individual, in most situations it is not necessary to reveal the source of the data by individual. This should happen only when it is essential to understand the data.
Communication	Selectively emphasizing parts or deemphasizing others can lead to misunderstandings and misinterpretation of the data.	It is important to present the data in a uniform, objective, and consistent manner.

(continued on page 134)

Table 9-1. Potential ethical problems encountered during program evaluations (continued).

Ethical Dilemma	Description	Possible Solution
Recommendations	Almost every evaluation study leads to specific recommendations. Sometimes, recommendations are based on subjective considerations recognizing the deficiencies or weaknesses as changes or improvements are explored.	Recommendations must be based on conclusions drawn from factual data analysis rather than opinions or biases.
Client Involvement	An ethical issue can surface when the client is involved in interpreting and understanding the data and drawing particular conclusions.	The extent to which the client is involved is important. The client needs to help set expectations, approve the evaluation plan, and review the data. Sometimes input is helpful but the client should not be able to influence the conclusions and recommendations.

perhaps, recommendations. Ultimately, actions on the recommendations will be taken.

4. *Remain independent.* As discussed earlier, it is important to remain independent from data sources, from the project itself, and from other relationships that might call into question the objectiveness of the evaluation.

5. *Emphasize process improvement.* All individuals need to understand that evaluation is designed to improve processes and not necessarily serve as a performance evaluation of the individuals who design, develop, deliver, or own the learning program.

A recommended resource for the evaluator is *Guiding Principles for Evaluators* (Shadish, 1995). These principles provide the evaluator general guidance on systematic inquiry, competence, integrity/honesty, respect for people, and responsibilities for general and public welfare. The American Evaluation Association (AEA) emphasizes that these principles, reprinted in figure 9-1, represent the official position of AEA on the topic of ethical practice (Russ-Eft & Preskill, 2001).

Standards for Evaluation

Evaluators need consistent processes and standard ways to collect, analyze, and report data. Although no standards have been formally developed for learning and development evaluation, standards have been developed for overall program evaluation. The American National Standards Institute (ANSI) and the Joint Committee on Standards for Educational Evaluation have published Program Evaluation Standards (figure 9-2). The setting for these standards is traditional program evaluation applied to public sector, where evaluation studies are conducted for health, public policy, education, and social programs.

Although the standards do not dictate what to do in different situations, they highlight the expectations and pitfalls of evaluation practice in the real world. They may add legitimacy to and support for evaluation studies. The context is different from some learning and development situations, but they serve as a trigger point for considerations.

It may be helpful to develop a very simple set of standards that can be used as guiding principles for a particular internal evaluation practice. Standards developed for use with the Kirkpatrick-Phillips five levels of evaluation follow. These standards have the

Figure 9-1. The American Evaluation Association's guiding principles for evaluators.

A. Systematic inquiry: Evaluators conduct systematic, data-based inquiries about whatever is being evaluated.

   1. Evaluators should adhere to the highest appropriate technical standards in conducting their work, whether that work is quantitative or qualitative in nature, so as to increase the accuracy and credibility of the evaluative information they produce.

   2. Evaluators should explore with the client the shortcomings and strengths both of the various evaluation questions it might be productive to ask and the various approaches that might be used for answering those questions.

   3. When presenting their work, evaluators should communicate their methods and approaches accurately and in sufficient detail to allow others to understand, interpret, and critique their work. They should make clear the limitations of an evaluation and its results. Evaluators should discuss in a contextually appropriate way those values, assumptions, theories, methods. These statements apply to all aspects of the evaluation, from its initial conceptualization to the eventual use of findings.

B. Competence: Evaluators provide competent performance to stakeholders.

   1. Evaluators should possess (or, here and elsewhere as appropriate, ensure that the evaluation team possess) the education, abilities, skills, and experience appropriate to undertake the tasks proposed in the evaluation.

   2. Evaluators should practice within the limits of their professional training and competence and should decline to conduct evaluations that fall substantially outside those limits. When declining the commission or request is not feasible or appropriate, evaluators should make clear any significant limitations on the evaluation that might result. Evaluators should make every effort to gain the competence directly or through the assistance of others who possess the required expertise.

   3. Evaluators should continually seek to maintain and improve their competencies, in order to provide the highest level of performance in their evaluations. This continuing professional development might include formal coursework and workshops, self-study, evaluations of one's own practice, and working with other evaluators to learn from their skills and expertise.

C. Integrity/honesty: Evaluators ensure the honesty and integrity of the entire evaluation process.

   1. Evaluators should negotiate honestly with clients and relevant stakeholders concerning the costs, tasks to be undertaken, limitations of methodology, scope of results likely to be obtained, and uses of data resulting from a specific evaluation. It is primarily the evaluator's responsibility to initiate discussion and clarification of these matters, not the client's.

   2. Evaluators should record all changes made in the originally negotiated project plans, and the reasons why the changes were made. If those changes would significantly affect the scope and likely results of the evaluation, the evaluator should inform the client and other important stakeholders in a timely fashion (barring good reason to the contrary, before proceeding with further work) of the changes and their likely impact.

   3. Evaluators should seek to determine, and where appropriate be explicit about, their own, their clients', and other stakeholders' interests concerning the conduct and outcomes of an evaluation (including financial, political, and career interests).

   4. Evaluators should disclose any roles or relationships they have concerning whatever is being evaluated that might pose a significant conflict of interest with their role as an evaluator. Any such conflict should be mentioned in reports of the evaluation results.

   5. Evaluators should not misrepresent their procedures, data, or findings. Within reasonable limits, they should attempt to prevent or correct any substantial misuses of their work by others.

   6. If evaluators determine that certain procedures or activities seem likely to produce misleading evaluative information or conclusions, they have the responsibility to communicate their concerns, and the reasons for them, to the client (the one who funds or requests the evaluation). If discussions with the client do not resolve these concerns, so that a misleading evaluation is then implemented, the evaluator may legitimately decline to conduct the evaluation if that is feasible and appropriate. If not, the evaluator should consult colleagues or relevant stakeholders about other proper ways to proceed (options might include, but are not limited to, discussions at a higher level, a dissenting cover letter or appendix, or refusal to sign the final document).

   7. Barring compelling reason to the contrary, evaluators should disclose all sources of financial support for an evaluation, and the source of the request for the evaluation.

D. Respect for people: Evaluators respect the security, dignity, and self-worth of the respondents, program participants, clients, and other stakeholders with whom they interact.

   1. Where applicable, evaluators must abide by current professional ethics and standards regarding risks, harms, and burdens that might be engendered to those participating in the evaluation; regarding informed consent for participation in evaluation, and regarding informing participants about the scope and limits of confidentiality. Examples of such standards include federal

(continued on page 136)

Figure 9-1. The American Evaluation Association's guiding principles for evaluators (continued).

regulations about protection of human subjects, or the ethical principles of such associations as the American Anthropological Association, the American Educational Research Association, or the American Psychological Association. Although this principle is not intended to extend the applicability of such ethics and standards beyond their current scope, evaluators should abide by them where it is feasible and desirable to do so.

2. Because justified negative or critical conclusions from an evaluation must be explicitly stated, evaluations sometimes produce results that harm client or stakeholder interests. Under this circumstance, evaluators should seek to maximize the benefits and reduce any unnecessary harms that might occur, provided this will not compromise the integrity of the evaluation findings. Evaluators should carefully judge when the benefits from doing the evaluation or in performing certain evaluation procedures should be forgone because of the risks or harms. Where possible, these issues should be anticipated during the negotiation of the evaluation.

3. Knowing that evaluations often will negatively affect the interests of some stakeholders, evaluators should conduct the evaluation and communicate its results in a way that clearly respects the stakeholders' dignity and self-worth.

4. Where feasible, evaluators should attempt to foster the social equity of the evaluation, so that those who give to the evaluation can receive some benefits in return. For example, evaluators should seek to ensure that those who bear the burdens of contributing data and incurring any risks are doing so willingly and that they have full knowledge of, and maximum feasible opportunity to obtain, any benefits that may be produced from the evaluation. When it would not endanger the integrity of the evaluation, respondents or program participants should be informed if and how they can receive services to which they are otherwise entitled without participating in the evaluation.

5. Evaluators have the responsibility to identify and respect differences among participants, such as differences in their culture, religion, gender, disability, age, sexual orientation, and ethnicity, and to be mindful of potential implications of these differences when planning, conducting, analyzing, and reporting their evaluations.

E. Responsibilities for general and public welfare: Evaluators articulate and take into account the diversity of interests and values that may be related to the general and public welfare.

1. When planning and reporting evaluations, evaluators should consider including important perspectives and interests of the full range of stakeholders in the object being evaluated. Evaluators should carefully consider the justification when omitting important value perspectives or the views of important groups.

2. Evaluators should consider not only the immediate operations and outcomes of whatever is being evaluated but also the broad assumptions, implications, and potential side effects of it.

3. Freedom of information is essential in a democracy. Hence, barring compelling reason to the contrary, evaluators should allow all relevant stakeholders to have access to evaluative information and should actively disseminate that information to stakeholders if resources allow. If different evaluation results are communicated in forms that are tailored to the interests of different stakeholders, those communications should ensure that each stakeholder group is aware of the existence of the other communications. Communications that are tailored to a given stakeholder should always include all important results that may bear interests of that stakeholder. In all cases, evaluators should strive to present results as clearly and simply as accuracy allows so that clients and other stakeholders can easily understand the evaluation process and results.

4. Evaluators should maintain a balance between client needs and other needs. Evaluators necessarily have a special relationship with the client who funds or requests the evaluation. By virtue of that relationship, evaluators must strive to meet legitimate client needs whenever it is feasible and appropriate to do so. However, that relationship can also place evaluators in difficult dilemmas when client interests conflict with other interests, or when client interests conflict with the obligation of evaluators for systematic inquiry, competence, integrity, and respect for people. In these cases, evaluators should explicitly identify and discuss the conflicts with the client and relevant stakeholders, resolve them when possible, determine whether continued work on the evaluation is advisable if the conflicts cannot be resolved, and make clear any significant limitations on the evaluation that might result if the conflict is not resolved.

5. Evaluators have obligations that encompass the public interest and good. These obligations are especially important when evaluators are supported by publicly generated funds, but clear threats to the public good should never be ignored in any evaluation. Because the public interest and good are rarely the same as the interests of any particular group (including those of the client or funding agency), evaluators will usually have to go beyond an analysis of particular stakeholder interests when considering the welfare of society as a whole.

Source: American Evaluation Association. (1995). "Guiding Principles for Evaluators: A Report From the AEA Task Force on Guiding Principles for Evaluators." http://www.eval.org/Guiding%20Principles.htm.

Figure 9-2. Program evaluation standards from the American Evaluation Association.

Utility

The utility standards are intended to ensure that an evaluation will serve the information needs of intended users.

U1 **Stakeholder Identification.** Persons involved in or affected by the evaluation should be identified, so that their needs can be addressed.

U2 **Evaluator Credibility.** The persons conducting the evaluation should be both trustworthy and competent to perform the evaluation, so that the evaluation findings achieve maximum credibility and acceptance.

U3 **Information Scope and Selection.** Information collected should be broadly selected to address pertinent questions about the program and be responsive to the needs and interests of clients and other specified stakeholders.

U4 **Values Identification.** The perspectives, procedures, and rationale used to interpret the findings should be carefully described, so that the bases for value judgments are clear.

U5 **Report Clarity.** Evaluation reports should clearly describe the program being evaluated, including its context, and the purposes, procedures, and findings of the evaluation, so that essential information is provided and easily understood.

U6 **Report Timeliness and Dissemination.** Significant interim findings and evaluation reports should be disseminated to intended users, so that they can be used in a timely fashion.

U7 **Evaluation Impact.** Evaluations should be planned, conducted, and reported in ways that encourage follow-through by stakeholders, so that the likelihood that the evaluation will be used is increased.

Feasibility

The feasibility standards are intended to ensure that an evaluation will be realistic, prudent, diplomatic, and frugal.

F1 **Practical Procedures.** The evaluation procedures should be practical to keep disruption to a minimum while needed information is obtained.

F2 **Political Viability.** The evaluation should be planned and conducted with anticipation of the different positions of various interest groups, so that their cooperation may be obtained, and so that possible attempts by any of these groups to curtail evaluation operations or to bias or misapply the results can be averted or counteracted.

F3 **Cost Effectiveness.** The evaluation should be efficient and produce information of sufficient value, so that the resources expended can be justified.

Propriety

The propriety standards are intended to ensure that an evaluation will be conducted legally, ethically, and with due regard for the welfare of those involved in the evaluation, as well as those affected by its results.

P1 **Service Orientation.** Evaluations should be designed to assist organizations to address and effectively serve the needs of the full range of targeted participants.

P2 **Formal Agreements.** Obligations of the formal parties to an evaluation (what is to be done, how, by whom, when) should be agreed to in writing, so that these parties are obligated to adhere to all conditions of the agreement or formally to renegotiate it.

P3 **Rights of Human Subjects.** Evaluations should be designed and conducted to respect and protect the rights and welfare of human subjects.

P4 **Human Interactions.** Evaluations should be designed and conducted to respect and protect the rights and welfare of human subjects.

P5 **Complete and Fair Assessment.** The evaluation should be complete and fair in its examination and recording of strengths and weaknesses of the program being evaluated, so that strengths can be built upon and problem areas addressed.

P6 **Disclosure and Findings.** The formal parties to an evaluation should ensure that the full set of evaluation findings along with pertinent limitations are made accessible to the persons affected by the evaluation, and any others with expressed legal rights to receive the results.

(continued on page 138)

Figure 9-2. Program evaluation standards from the American Evaluation Association (continued).

P7   **Conflict of Interest.** Conflict of interest should be dealt with openly and honestly, so that it does not compromise the evaluation processes and results.

P8   **Fiscal Responsibility.** The evaluator's allocation and expenditure of resources should reflect sound accountability procedures and otherwise be prudent and ethically responsible so that expenditures are accounted for and appropriate.

Accuracy

The accuracy standards are intended to ensure that an evaluation will reveal and convey technically adequate information about the features that determine worth or merit of the program being evaluated.

A1   **Program Documentation.** The program being evaluated should be described and documented clearly and accurately, so that the program is clearly identified.

A2   **Context Analysis.** The context in which the program exists should be examined in enough detail, so that its likely influences on the program can be identified.

A3   **Described Purposes and Procedures.** The purposes and procedures of the evaluation should be monitored and described in enough detail, so that they can be identified and assessed.

A4   **Defensible Information Sources.** The sources of information used in a program evaluation should be described in enough detail, so that the adequacy of the information can be assessed.

A5   **Valid Information.** The information gathering procedures should be chosen or developed and then implemented so that they will assure that the interpretation arrived at is valid for intended use.

A6   **Reliable Information.** The information gathering procedures should be chosen or developed and then implemented so that they will assure that the information obtained is sufficiently reliable for the intended use.

A7   **Systematic Information.** The information collected, processed, and reported in an evaluation should be systematically reviewed and any errors found should be corrected.

A8   **Analysis of Quantitative Information.** Quantitative information in an evaluation should be appropriately and systematically analyzed so that evaluation questions are effectively answered.

A9   **Analysis of Qualitative Information.** Qualitative information in an evaluation should be appropriately and systematically analyzed so that evaluation questions are effectively answered.

A10   **Justified Conclusions.** The conclusions reached in an evaluation should be explicitly justified, so that stakeholders can assess them.

A11   **Impartial Reporting.** Reporting procedures should guard against distortion caused by personal feelings and biases of any party to the evaluation, so that evaluation reports fairly reflect the evaluation findings.

A12   **Metaevaluation.** The evaluation itself should be formatively and summarily evaluated against these and other pertinent standards so that its conduct is appropriately guided and, on completion, stakeholders can closely examine its strengths and weaknesses.

Source: Ramlow, M.E. (1994). "The Program Evaluation Standards: Summary of the Standards." Fairhaven, MA: American Evaluation Association. http://www.eval.org/EvaluationDocuments/progeval.html. Reproduced with permission.

extra characteristic of being very conservative in the analysis. This additional conservatism brings the required credibility expected by audiences as the data from impact studies are presented.

1.   When a higher-level evaluation is conducted, data must be collected at lower

levels. The first standard requires data through the chain of impact on the five levels of evaluation. This chain of impact clearly shows the audience how reaction leads to learning leads to application leads to impact and ultimately leads to a negative or positive ROI at level 5. For organizations using this five-level framework, it is essential for all audiences to see the different levels of data so they can see the chain of impact in action.

2. When an evaluation is planned for a higher level, the previous level of evaluation does not have to be comprehensive. The second standard is based on the concept of saving resources. When a higher level of evaluation is selected, shortcuts can be taken at the lower levels. The corollary of this standard is that most of the money or efforts should be placed on the highest level of evaluation. If financial resources are not an issue, obviously comprehensive evaluation can be tackled all along at the different levels.

3. When collecting and analyzing data, use only the most credible source. This standard may seem obvious, but it requires reflection on the credibility of different sources of data. Whatever the use of the data, it is critical for that source to be credible and perceived to be credible in the organization.

4. When analyzing data, choose the most conservative analytical approach among the alternatives. This standard suggests that the alternative be selected that yields the lowest ROI. This is assuming, of course, that each alternative is equally credible. This conservative approach is gaining buy-in from your audience.

5. At least one method must be used to isolate the effects of the solution. A difficult challenge is the issue of isolating effects of the learning solution. When evaluations are conducted with impact data and ROI data (levels 4 and 5), it is essential to isolate the effects of the learning solution or processes to gain immediate credibility of the analysis. Otherwise, the study may be invalid and virtually worthless because there is no connection to the business result.

6. If no improvement data is available for a population or from a specific source, it is assumed that little or no improvement has occurred. This standard takes an ultraconservative approach to missing data: No data equals no improvement. If a group of participants does not provide data or if the individuals are no longer in the job generating data for improvement, it is assumed that there was no value or no improvement for the duration of the study. This standard allows the evaluator to avoid the issue of statistical inference about the population and requires the project to pay off based on the data available.

7. Estimates of improvements should be adjusted (discounted) for the potential error of the estimate. Sometimes estimates are used in the analysis. When they are, they should be adjusted for the potential error of the estimate. The adjustment is a way of reducing the value, in essence, discounting the results for the potential error.

8. Extreme data items and unsupported claims should not be used in ROI calculations. Although this standard is somewhat subjective, it forces the evaluator to define what is considered to be extreme data and to automatically omit from the analysis unsupported claims or at least put the unsupported claims in a separate category. These two actions involved in the data analysis add to the credibility of the process.

9. Only the first year of benefits (annual) should be used in the ROI analysis of short-term solutions. For most learning and development programs, one year of data should be used to show the value of the improvement. In most cases, data will actually be collected in the two- to six-month timeframe after a learning program is implemented. That data is extrapolated for an entire year to yield the first year of benefits. For longer-term programs, the

data must be collected for longer periods. An important point is to keep it conservative, be fair to the project, and fit the timeframe that executives would think appropriate.

10. Costs of the solution should be fully loaded for ROI analysis. This principle focuses on the cost of the project and requires that all costs—both indirect and direct—be included in the analysis. In some cases, this may be excessively loading the costs; however, if a cost is connected in any way to the program, it is best to include it in the analysis if costs are compared to the actual monetary benefits (ROI).

11. Intangible measures are defined as measures that are purposely not converted to monetary values. If an intangible data item cannot be credibly converted to monetary value, it is left as an intangible. There are usually some very precise guidelines for making these conversions.

12. The results from the ROI Methodology must be communicated to all key stakeholders. Four target audience are required always: the participants (if they provided data), the immediate managers of the participants, the sponsor (key client), and the learning and development staff. Others may need to know based on their involvement in the program.

These standards illustrate the need for guidelines in analysis to ensure that projects are conducted the same way from one study to another. They ensure that the key audiences, such as executives, understand that there are some conservative rules in developing studies. Additional details on these standards can be found in other works (J.J. Phillips, 2003).

Final Thoughts

This chapter provided ethical guidance to keep relationships and projects on track. The evaluator must judge situations and make decisions regarding ethical issues. To increase ethical sensitivity, the evaluator can use the following framework of questions (Zinn, 1993). Answering yes to the questions may indicate that the evaluator is facing an ethical dilemma:

- Is there any question of legality or of violating professional standards or codes of ethics?
- Will there be potential harm to anyone as a result of my decision/action, or of my failure to act?
- When I (or others) talk about this matter, do we use key words or phrases, such as right or wrong, black or white, fair or unfair, bottom line, should, appropriate, ethical, conflict, or values?
- Am I concerned about my decision being equally fair to all parties?
- Do I feel a conflict between my personal values and professional interests (for example, organizational goals or client needs)?
- Is there any controversy or strong opposition regarding this decision?
- Will I be hesitant to reveal my decision about this matter to others? Would I take the same action in a "clean, well-lit room"?
- Do I have a gut feeling that something is not quite right about this?
- Is this a decision that nobody else wants to make?

Asking these questions and using the guidance provided in this chapter avoids ethical situations, and this is the ethical goal for the evaluator. Standards are necessary to have a consistent and credible evaluation process. The recommendation is to develop a simple set of standards and use them routinely.

Appendix A

How Results-Based Are Your Training and Performance Improvement Programs? An Assessment Survey for Managers

Overview

The amount of management support needed for organization development, performance improvement, training and development, and human resource development programs is very critical to their success. In most situations the amount of support managers are willing to provide is directly linked to their perception of the effectiveness of the programs. If the programs are achieving results and helping the organization reach its goals, managers are often willing to support the programs, provide resources to make them successful, reinforce specific behavioral objectives, and become more actively involved in the process.

The following instrument provides an assessment of the extent to which managers perceive that programs are achieving results. It provides the organization with an assessment of the effectiveness of performance improvement, training and development, human resource development, and organization development as perceived by the managers.

Use

The instrument can be used in the following ways:

- It can serve as a benchmark for specific efforts, events, and activities aimed at enhancing the level of support.

- In efforts to increase the effectiveness of programs, this instrument will serve as a periodic assessment of the progress made.
- It can serve as a useful discussion tool in workshops for managers where the goal is to enhance their support for the training, performance improvement, or organizational development function.
- It is a helpful tool to compare one group of managers in a division, plant, region, or subsidiary company with others to determine where specific attention may be needed.

Target Audience

The target audience for the instrument is middle and upper managers who provide support to the performance improvement, training and development, and organizational development function. These are the managers in the organization who can influence the success of those efforts.

Administration

The instrument should be administered without discussion. Participants and managers should be instructed to provide very candid responses. The results should be quickly tabulated by the respondents and discussed and interpreted in a group discussion.

Training and Development Programs Assessment: A Survey for Managers.

Instructions

For each of the following statements, please circle the response that best matches the Training and Development function at your organization. If none of the answers describe the situation, select the one that best fits. Please be candid with your responses.

1. The direction of the Training and Development function at your organization:

   a) Shifts with requests, problems, and changes as they occur.
   b) Is determined by human resources and adjusted as needed.
   c) Is based on a mission and a strategic plan for the function.

2. The primary mode of operation of the Training and Development function is:

   a) To respond to requests by managers and other employees to deliver training programs and services.
   b) To help management react to crisis situations and reach solutions through training programs and services.
   c) To implement many training programs in collaboration with management to prevent problems and crisis situations.

3. The goals of the Training and Development function are:

   a) Set by the training staff based on perceived demand for programs.
   b) Developed consistent with human resources plans and goals.
   c) Developed to integrate with operating goals and strategic plans of the organization.

4. Most new programs are initiated:

   a) By request of top management.
   b) When a program appears to be successful in another organization.
   c) After a needs analysis has indicated that the program is needed.

5. When a major organizational change is made:

   a) We decide only which presentations are needed, not which skills are needed.
   b) We occasionally assess what new skills and knowledge are needed.
   c) We systematically evaluate what skills and knowledge are needed.

6. To define training plans:

   a) Management is asked to choose training from a list of canned, existing courses.
   b) Employees are asked about their training needs.
   c) Training needs are systematically derived from a thorough analysis of performance problems.

7. When determining the timing of training and the target audiences:

   a) We have lengthy, nonspecific training courses for large audiences.
   b) We tie specific training needs to specific individuals and groups.
   c) We deliver training almost immediately before its use, and it is given only to those people who need it.

8. The responsibility for results from training:

   a) Rests primarily with the training staff to ensure that the programs are successful.
   b) Is a responsibility of the training staff and line managers, who jointly ensure that results are obtained.
   c) Is a shared responsibility of the training staff, participants, and managers all working together to ensure success.

9. Systematic, objective evaluation, designed to ensure that trainees are performing appropriately on the job:

   a) Is never accomplished. The only evaluations are during the program and they focus on how much the participants enjoyed the program.
   b) Is occasionally accomplished. Participants are asked if the training was effective on the job.
   c) Is frequently and systematically pursued. Performance is evaluated after training is completed.

10. New programs are developed:

   a) Internally, using a staff of instructional designers and specialists.
   b) By vendors. We usually purchase programs modified to meet the organization's needs.
   c) In the most economical and practical way to meet deadlines and cost objectives, using internal staff and vendors.

11. Costs for training and OD are accumulated:

   a) On a total aggregate basis only.
   b) On a program-by-program basis.
   c) By specific process components such as development and delivery, in addition to a specific program.

12. Management involvement in the training process is:

   a) Very low with only occasional input.
   b) Moderate, usually by request, or on an as-needed basis.
   c) Deliberately planned for all major training activities, to ensure a partnership arrangement.

13. To ensure that training is transferred into performance on the job, we:

   a) Encourage participants to apply what they have learned and report results.
   b) Ask managers to support and reinforce training and report results.
   c) Utilize a variety of training transfer strategies appropriate for each situation.

14. The training staff's interaction with line management is:

   a) Rare, we almost never discuss issues with them.
   b) Occasional, during activities such as needs analysis or program coordination.
   c) Regular, to build relationships, as well as to develop and deliver programs.

15. Training and Development's role in major change efforts is:

   a) To conduct training to support the project, as required.
   b) To provide administrative support for the program, including training.
   c) To initiate the program, coordinate the overall effort, and measures its progress—in addition to providing training.

16. Most managers view the Training and Development function as:

   a) A questionable function that wastes too much time of employees.
   b) A necessary function that probably cannot be eliminated.
   c) An important resource that can be used to improve the organization.

17. Training and Development programs are:

   a) Activity-oriented. (All supervisors attend the "Performance Appraisal Workshop.")
   b) Individual results-based. (The participant will reduce his or her error rate by at least 20%.)
   c) Organizational results-based. (The cost of quality will decrease by 25%.)

18. The investment in Training and Development is measured primarily by:

   a) Subjective opinions.
   b) Observations by management, reactions from participants.
   c) Dollar return through improved productivity, cost savings, or better quality.

19. The Training and Development effort consists of:

   a) Usually one-shot, seminar-type approaches.
   b) A full array of courses to meet individual needs.
   c) A variety of training and development programs implemented to bring about change in the organization.

(continued on page 144)

Training and Development Programs Assessment: A Survey for Managers (continued).

20. New Training and Development programs, without some formal method of evaluation, are implemented at my organization:

    a) Regularly.
    b) Seldom.
    c) Never.

21. The results of training programs are communicated:

    a) When requested, to those who have a need to know.
    b) Occasionally, to members of management only.
    c) Routinely, to a variety of selected target audiences.

22. Management involvement in training evaluation:

    a) Is minor, with no specific responsibilities and few requests.
    b) Consists of informal responsibilities for evaluation, with some requests for formal training.
    c) Very specific. All managers have some responsibilities in evaluation.

23. During a business decline at my organization, the training function will:

    a) Be the first to have its staff reduced.
    b) Be retained at the same staffing level.
    c) Go untouched in staff reductions and possibly beefed up.

24. Budgeting for Training and Development is based on:

    a) Last year's budget.
    b) Whatever the training department can "sell."
    c) A zero-based system.

25. The principal group that must justify Training and Development expenditures is:

    a) The Training and Development department.
    b) The human resources or administrative function.
    c) Line management.

26. Over the last two years, the Training and Development budget as a percent of operating expenses has:

    a) Decreased.
    b) Remained stable.
    c) Increased.

27. Top management's involvement in the implementation of Training and Development programs:

    a) Is limited to sending invitations, extending congratulations, passing out certificates, and so forth.
    b) Includes monitoring progress, opening/closing speeches, presentation on the outlook of the organization, and so forth.
    c) Includes program participation to see what's covered, conducting major segments of the program, requiring key executives to be involved, and so forth.

28. Line management involvement in conducting training and development programs is:

    a) Very minor; only HRD specialists conduct programs.
    b) Limited to a few specialists conducting programs in their area of expertise.
    c) Significant. On the average, over half of the programs are conducted by key line managers.

29. When an employee completes a training program and returns to the job, his or her supervisor is likely to:

    a) Make no reference to the program.
    b) Ask questions about the program and encourage the use of the material.
    c) Require use of the program material and give positive rewards when the material is used successfully.

30. When an employee attends an outside seminar, upon return, he or she is required to:

    a) Do nothing.
    b) Submit a report summarizing the program.
    c) Evaluate the seminar, outline plans for implementing the material covered, and estimate the value of the program.

Interpreting the Training and Development Program Assessment

Score the assessment instrument as follows. Allow

- 1 point for each (a) response
- 3 points for each (b) response
- 5 points for each (c) response.

The total will be between 30 and 150 points. The interpretation of the scoring is provided below. The explanation is based on the input from dozens of organizations and hundreds of managers.

Score Range	Analysis of Score
120–150	*Outstanding Environment* for achieving results with Training and Development. Great management support. A truly successful example of results-based Training and Development.
90–119	*Above Average* in achieving results with Training and Development. Good management support. A solid and methodical approach to results-based Training and Development.
60–89	*Needs Improvement* to achieve desired results with Training and Development. Management support is ineffective. Training and Development programs do not usually focus on results.
30–59	*Serious Problems* with the success and status of Training and Development. Management support is nonexistent. Training and Development programs are not producing results.

Source: Phillips, J.J. (1997). *Handbook of Training Evaluation and Measurement Methods,* 3rd edition. Boston: Butterworth-Heinemann. Reprinted with permission.

References

American Evaluation Association. (1995). "Guiding Principles for Evaluators: A Report From the AEA Task Force on Guiding Principles for Evaluators." http://www.eval.org/EvaluationDocuments/aeaprin6.html.

Bell, C.R., and H. Shea. (1998). *Dance Lessons: Six Steps to Great Partnerships in Business and Life.* San Francisco: Berrett-Koehler.

Bernthal, P.R., K. Colteryahn, P. Davis, J. Naughton, W. Rothwell, and R. Wellins. (2004). *ASTD Competency Study: Mapping the Future.* Alexandria, VA: ASTD.

Blanchard, K. (2002, October). ASTD Global Forum. Berlin, Germany.

Block, P. (2000). *Flawless Consulting,* 2nd edition. San Francisco: Jossey-Bass/Pfeiffer.

Broad, M.L. (editor). (1997). *In Action: Transferring Learning to the Workplace.* Alexandria, VA: ASTD.

Brogden, H.E. (1946). "On the Interpretation of the Correlation Coefficient as a Measure of Predictive Efficiency." *Journal of Educational Psychology, 37,* 65–76.

Brogden, H.E. (1949). "When Testing Pays Off." *Personnel Psychology, 2,* 171–183.

Burkett, H. (2001). "Program Process Improvement." *In Action: Measuring Return on Investment, 3,* 37–64. Alexandria, VA: ASTD.

Devany, M. (2001). "Measuring ROI of Computer Training in a Small to Medium-Sized Enterprise." In: P.P. Phillips (editor), *In Action: Measuring Return on Investment,* 185–196. Alexandria, VA: ASTD.

Drimmer, A. (2002). *Reframing the Measurement Debate: Moving Beyond Program Analysis in the Learning Function.* Washington, DC: Corporate Executive Board.

Falletta, S.V., and J.M. Lamb. (1998). "Measuring and Evaluating Training at the Technical Education Centers." In: J.J. Phillips (editor), *In Action: Implementing Evaluation Systems and Processes.* Alexandria, VA: ASTD.

Hodges, T. (1998). "Measuring Training Throughout the Bell Atlantic Organization." In: J.J. Phillips (editor), *In Action: Implementing Evaluation Systems and Processes.* Alexandria, VA: ASTD.

Hodges, T.K. (2002). *Linking Learning and Performance: A Practical Guide to Measuring Learning and On-the-Job Application.* Boston: Butterworth-Heinemann.

Kaplan, R.S., and D.P. Norton. (1992, January–February). "The Balanced Scorecard: Measures that Drive Performance." *Harvard Business Review,* 71–79.

Kirkpatrick, D. (1998). *Evaluating Training Programs: The Four Levels,* 2nd edition. San Francisco: Berrett-Koehler Publishers.

Mariotti, J.L. (1996). *The Power of Partnerships: The Next Step Beyond TQM, Reengineering and Lean Production.* Oxford, England: Basil Blackwell.

McLagan, P. (1989). *The Models.* Alexandria, VA: ASTD.

Newman, D.L., and R.D. Brown. (1992). "Violations of Evaluation Standards." *Evaluation Review, 16*(3).

Phillips, J.J. (1997). *Handbook of Training Evaluation and Measurement Methods,* 3rd edition. Woburn, MA: Butterworth-Heinemann.

Phillips, J.J. (2000). *The Consultant's Scorecard: Tracking Results and Bottom-Line Impact of Consulting Projects.* New York: McGraw-Hill.

Phillips, J.J. (2003). *Return on Investment in Training and Performance Improvement Programs,* 2nd edition. Woburn, MA: Butterworth-Heinemann.

Phillips, J.J. (series editor), and D.J. Mitch (editor). (2002). *In Action: Coaching for Extraordinary Results.* Alexandria, VA: ASTD.

Phillips, J.J., and P.P. Phillips. (1999). "Level 5 Evaluation: Mastering ROI," *Infoline,* No. 259805. Alexandria, VA: ASTD.

Phillips, J.J. (series editor), and P.P. Phillips (editor). (2001). *In Action: Measuring Return on Investment,* volume 3. Alexandria, VA: ASTD.

Phillips, J.J. (series editor), and P.P. Phillips (editor). (2002a). *In Action: Retaining Your Best Employees.* Alexandria, VA: ASTD and the Society for Human Resource Management.

Phillips, J.J. (series editor), and P.P. Phillips (editor). (2002b). *In Action: Measuring ROI in the Public Sector.* Alexandria, VA: ASTD.

Phillips, J.J. (series editor), and L. Schmidt (editor). (2003). *In Action: Implementing Training Scorecards.* Alexandria, VA: ASTD.

Phillips, J.J., and L. Schmidt. (2004). *The Leadership Scorecard.* Boston: Butterworth-Heinemann.

Phillips, J.J., and R.D. Stone. (2002). *How to Measure Training Results: A Practical Guide for Tracking the Six Key Indicators.* New York: McGraw-Hill.

Phillips, J.J., R.D. Stone, and P.P. Phillips. (2001). *The Human Resources Scorecard: Measuring the Return on Investment.* Woburn, MA: Butterworth-Heinemann.

Phillips, P.P. (2002). *The Bottomline on ROI: Basics, Benefits, and Barriers to Measuring Training and Performance Improvement.* Atlanta: CEP Press and Silver Spring, MD: ISPI.

Phillips, P.P. (2003). *Training Evaluation in the Public Sector.* Unpublished dissertation. The University of Southern Mississippi. International Development.

Phillips, P.P., and H. Burkett. (2001, November). "Managing Evaluation Shortcuts." *Infoline,* No. 25011. Alexandria, VA: ASTD.

Phillips, P.P., and H. Burkett. (in press). *The ROI Fieldbook.* Woburn, MA: Butterworth-Heinemann.

Phillips, P.P., C. Gaudet, and J.J. Phillips. (2003, April). "Evaluation Data: Planning and Use." *Infoline,* No. 250304. Alexandria, VA: ASTD.

Ramlow, M.E. (1994). "The Program Evaluation Standards: Summary of the Standards." Fairhaven, MA: American Evaluation Association. http://www.eval.org/EvaluationDocuments/progeval.html.

Rothwell, W.J. (1996). *ASTD Models for Human Performance Improvement.* Alexandria, VA: ASTD.

Rothwell, W.J., C.K. Hohne, and S. King. (2000). *Human Performance: Building Practitioner Competence.* Boston: Butterworth-Heinemann.

Russ-Eft, D., and H. Preskill. (2001). *Evaluation in Organizations: A Systematic Approach to Enhancing Learning, Performance, and Change.* Cambridge, MA: Perseus Publishing.

Schmidt, L. (editor). (2003). *Implementing Training Scorecards.* Alexandria, VA: ASTD.

Shadish, W.R. (1995). *Guiding Principles for Evaluators (New Directions for Program Evaluation),* no. 66. New York: John Wiley & Sons.

Sutcliffe, K.M., and K. Weber. (2003, May). "The High Cost of Accurate Knowledge." *Harvard Business Review, 62,* 74–82.

Tsutsumi, U., and S. Kubota. (2003). *In Action: Implementing Training Scorecards.* In: L. Schmidt (editor) and J.J. Phillips (series editor). Alexandria, VA.: ASTD.

U.S. Government Accountability Office. (2003). *Human Capital: Guide for Strategic Training and Development Efforts.* GAO-03-893G. Washington, DC: GAO.

Wall, S., and E. White. (1997). "Building Saturn's Organization-wide Transfer Support Model." In: M. Broad (editor), *Transferring Learning to the Workplace,* 165–188.

Zinn, L.M. (1993). "Do the Right Thing: Ethical Decision Making in Professional and Business Practice." *Adult Learning* 5(2): 7–8.

Additional Resources

Many additional resources are available to help you understand, use, and implement evaluation in your organization. The materials listed below are available directly from the publishers or can be purchased on Amazon.com or from other bookstores.

Books (by Year of Publication)

The Success Case Method. Robert O. Brinkerhoff. San Francisco: Berrett-Koehler Publishers. 2003.

Project Management Scorecard: Measuring the Success of Project Management Solutions. J.J. Phillips, Timothy W. Bothell, and G. Lynne Snead. Woburn, MA: Butterworth-Heinemann. 2002.

Rapid Evaluation. Susan Barksdale and Teri Lund. Alexandria, VA: ASTD. 2001.

The Targeted Evaluation Process. Wendy L. Combs and Salvatore V. Falleta. Alexandria, VA: ASTD. 2000.

Evaluating Training. Sharon Bartrow and Brenda Gibson. Amherst, MA: HRD Press. 1999.

Measurit: Achieving Profitable Training. Marsha Mondschein. Leawood, KS: Leathers Publishing. 1999.

Results: How to Assess Performance, Learning, and Perceptions in Organizations. Richard A. Swanson and Elwood F. Holton, III. San Francisco: Berrett-Koehler. 1999.

Evaluating Corporate Training: Models and Issues. Stephen M. Brown and Constance J. Seidner. Boston: Kluwer Academic Publishers. 1998.

Evaluating the Impact of Training. Scott B. Parry. Alexandria, VA: ASTD. 1997.

Establishing the Value of Training. Sharon G. Fisher and Barbara J. Ruffind. Amherst, MA: HRD Press. 1996.

Evaluating Training Effectiveness, 2nd edition. Peter Bramley. London: McGraw-Hill. 1996.

Evaluating Human Resources, Programs, and Organizations. Byron R. Burnham. Malabar, FL: Krieger Publishing. 1995.

The Learning Alliance. R.O. Brinkerhoff and S.J. Gill. San Francisco: Jossey-Bass. 1994.

Flex: A Flexible Tool for Continuously Improving Your Evaluation of Training Effectiveness. Gary Schouborg. Amherst, MA: HRD Press. 1993.

Make Training Worth Every Penny. Jane Holcomb. San Diego: Pfeiffer & Company. 1992.

The Training Evaluation Process. David J. Basarab, Sr., and Darrell K. Root. Norwell, MA: Kluwer Academic Publishers. 1992.

Training Evaluation Handbook. A.C. Newby. San Diego: Pfeiffer & Company. 1992.

Evaluation: A Tool for Improving HRD Quality. Nancy M. Dixon. San Diego: University Associates. 1990.

Training for Impact. Dana Gaines Robinson and James C. Robinson. San Francisco: Jossey-Bass. 1989.

Achieving Results from Training. Robert O. Brinkerhoff. San Francisco: Jossey-Bass. 1987.

Evaluating Employee Training Programs. Elizabeth M. Hawthorne. New York: Quorum Books. 1987.

How to Measure Training Effectiveness. Leslie Rae. New York: Nichols Publishing Company. 1986.

Evaluating Job-Related Training. Basil S. Deming. Alexandria, VA: ASTD. 1982.

Evaluation of Management Training. Peter Warr, Michael Bird, and Neil Rackham. London: Gower Press Ltd. 1970.

Case Studies (by Year of Publication)

In Action: Implementing Training Scorecards. L. Schmidt, editor; J.J. Phillips, series editor. Alexandria, VA: ASTD. 2003.

In Action: Measuring ROI in the Public Sector. P.P. Phillips, editor; J.J. Phillips, series editor. Alexandria, VA: ASTD. 2002.

In Action: Measuring Intellectual Capital. P.P. Phillips, editor; J.J. Phillips, series editor. Alexandria, VA: ASTD, 2002.

In-Action: Implementing E-Learning Solutions. C. Pope, editor; J.J. Phillips, series editor. Alexandria, VA: ASTD. 2001.

In Action: Measuring Return on Investment on Interactive Selling Skills, 3. P.P. Phillips, editor; J.J. Phillips, series editor. Alexandria, VA: ASTD. 2001.

In Action: Performance Analysis and Consulting. J.J. Phillips, series editor. Alexandria, VA: ASTD. 2000.

In Action: Measuring Learning and Performance. T.K. Hodges, editor; J.J. Phillips, series editor. Alexandria, VA: ASTD. 1999.

In Action: Implementing Evaluation Systems and Processes. J.J. Phillips, series editor. Alexandria, VA: ASTD. 1998.

In Action: Implementing Evaluation Systems and Processes. J.J. Phillips, series editor. Alexandria, VA: ASTD. 1998.

In Action: Transferring Learning to the Workplace. M.L. Broad, editor; J.J. Phillips, series editor. Alexandria, VA: ASTD. 1997.

In Action: Conducting Needs Assessment. J.J. Phillips and E. F. Holton, III, editors. Alexandria, VA: ASTD. 1995.

In Action: Measuring Return on Investment, 1. J.J. Phillips, series editor. Alexandria, VA: ASTD. 1994.

Infoline: The How-To Reference Tool for Training and Performance Professionals

The *Infoline* series from ASTD offers a variety of brief publications with tools, templates, and job aids included. The following issues of *Infoline* focus on each of the five levels of evaluation discussed in this book:

Issue 259008: "How to Collect Data." J.W. Gilley, author; B. Darraugh, editor.

Issue 258612: "Surveys from Start to Finish." L. Long, author; G. Spruell, editor.

Issue 258907: "Testing for Learning Outcomes." D.G. Hacker, author; C. Sharpe, editor.

Issue 259705: "Essentials for Evaluation." A.K. Waagen, author; C. Sharpe, editor.

Issue 259709: "Evaluating Technical Training: A Functional Approach." S.V. Falletta and W.L. Combs, authors; C. Sharpe, editor.

Issue 259813: "Level 1 Evaluation: Reaction and Planned Action." (1999). J.J. Phillips, author; C. Sharpe, editor.

Issue 259814: "Level 2 Evaluation: Learning." (1999). J.J. Phillips, author; C. Sharpe, editor.

Issue 259815: "Level 3 Evaluation: Application." (1999). J.J. Phillips, author; C. Sharpe, editor.

Issue 259816: "Level 4 Evaluation: Business Results." (1999). J.J. Phillips and R.D. Stone, authors; C. Sharpe, editor.

Issue 259805: "Level 5 Evaluation: Mastering ROI." (1998, 2000). J.J. Phillips and P. Pulliam, authors; C. Sharpe, editor.

Issue 250111: "Managing Evaluation Shortcuts." (November 2001). P.P. Phillips and H. Burkett, authors.

Issue 250304: "Evaluation Data: Planning and Use." (April 2003). P.P. Phillips, C. Gaudet, and J.J. Phillips, authors.

Software

Software has been developed to support evaluation as described in this book. The most complete system of measurement that provides various ways to analyze data at levels 1 through 5 uses a process called Metrics that Matter. This is a comprehensive measurement tool to bring accountability to the overall training and learning function.

Another option is a variety of routines and features to develop specific impact studies. This version can also be used for impact studies as a stand-alone product. Both products are available on a subscription basis. Additional details can be obtained from KnowledgeAdvisors (www.knowledgeadvisors.com).

Because of the variety and constantly changing nature of software to support evaluation, a complete list of software is not provided here. An updated list of current tools is available directly from the authors.

About the Authors

Jack J. Phillips

As a world-renowned expert on measurement and evaluation, Dr. Jack J. Phillips is chairman of the ROI Institute. Through the Institute, Phillips provides consulting services for *Fortune* 500 companies and workshops for major conference providers throughout the world. Phillips is also the author or editor of more than 30 books and more than 100 articles.

His expertise in measurement and evaluation is based on more than 27 years of corporate experience in five industries (aerospace, textiles, metals, construction materials, and banking). Phillips has served as training and development manager at two *Fortune* 500 firms, senior HR officer at two firms, president of a regional federal savings bank, and management professor at a major state university.

His background in training and HR led Phillips to develop the ROI Process—a revolutionary process that provides bottom-line figures and accountability for all types of training, performance improvement, human resources, and technology programs.

Books most recently written by Phillips include *The Leadership Scorecard* (with L. Schmidt, Butterworth-Heinemann, 2004); *How to Measure Training Results* (with R.D. Stone, McGraw-Hill, 2002); *The Human Resources Scorecard: Measuring Return on Investment* (with R.D. Stone and P.P. Phillips, Butterworth-Heinemann, 2001); *The Consultant's Scorecard: Tracking Results and Bottom-Line Impact of Consulting Projects* (McGraw-Hill, 2000); *HRD Trends Worldwide: Shared Solutions to Compete in a Global Economy* (Butterworth-Heinemann, 1999); *Return on Investment in Training and Performance Improvement Programs* (Butterworth-Heinemann, 2003); *Handbook of Training Evaluation and Measurement Methods,* 3rd edition (Butterworth-Heinemann, 1997); and *Accountability in Human Resource Management* (Butterworth-Heinemann, 1996). Phillips is series editor for ASTD's *In Action* casebook series and also serves as series editor for Butterworth-Heinemann's *Improving Human Performance* series.

Phillips earned undergraduate degrees in electrical engineering, physics, and mathematics, a master's degree in decision sciences from Georgia State University, and a doctoral degree in human resource management from the University of Alabama.

Patricia Pulliam Phillips

Patti Phillips is an internationally recognized author, consultant, and researcher. She is president and CEO of the ROI Institute, the leading source of ROI evaluation education, research, and networking. She is a chairman of the Chelsea Group, an international consulting organization supporting organizations and their efforts to build accountability into their training, human resources, and performance improvement programs. She helps organizations implement the ROI Methodology in countries around the world including South Africa, Singapore, Japan, New Zealand, Australia, Italy, Turkey, France, Germany, Canada, and the United States.

Phillips has always had an interest in accountability and evaluation, which has been manifested throughout her academic career and years of corporate life. During her tenure as a corporate manager who observed performance improvement initiatives from the client perspective, results were imperative. As manager of market planning and research, she was responsible for the development of marketing programs for residential and commercial customers. In this role, she played an integral part in establishing Marketing University, a learning environment that supported the needs of new sales and marketing representatives.

In 1997, Phillips took advantage of an opportunity to pursue a career in a growing consulting business at which time she was introduced to training, human resources, and performance improvement from a new perspective that directly reflected her values of accountability—ROI evaluation. Since 1997, she has embraced the ROI Methodology by committing herself to ongoing research and practice. To that end, she has implemented ROI in private-sector and public-sector organizations by conducting ROI impact studies on programs such as leadership development, sales, new-hire orientation, and human performance improvement programs. She works with corporations, government, and academia to broaden the application of ROI evaluation to programs directly influencing the economic growth of communities around the world.

Phillips's academic accomplishments include a doctoral degree in international development and a master's degree of arts in public and private management. She is certified in ROI evaluation and has been awarded the designation of certified performance technologist.

Her most recent publications include *The Bottomline on ROI* (Center for Effective Performance, 2002), which won 2003 ISPI Award of Excellence; *The Human Resources Scorecard: Measuring Return on Investment* (Butterworth-Heinemann, 2001); and several of ASTD's *In Action* casebooks, including *Measuring Return on Investment*, volume 3 (2001),

Measuring ROI in the Public Sector (2002), and *Retaining Your Best Employees* (2002). She has also written several articles for ASTD's *Infoline* series on evaluation and ROI. She is published in a variety of journals, serves as adjunct faculty teaching training evaluation, and speaks on the subject at conferences including ASTD's International Conference and Exposition and the ISPI International Conference.

Toni Krucky Hodges

Toni Hodges has more than 23 years of experience measuring the impact of human performance. She has conducted and managed operational, systems, and group evaluations for corporate, defense contracting, and government organizations. Her work has included the development of individual assessment tools as well as large organizational tracking tools, all aimed at measuring the performance and monetary value of human resource and systems intervention programs.

At Bell Atlantic she established and managed an award-winning evaluation program, recognized for "innovated performance in the area of the Corporate University: Measuring the Impact of Learning." The selection for the award was made by a consortium of organizations around the country. She is a certified ROI professional and received the Practitioner of the Year award from the ROI Network in 2000. She was profiled as one of Training's New Guard by ASTD in 2001.

Since leaving corporate service, she has been assisting large and small organizations in the United States and Canada with ROI impact studies, setting up evaluation programs from scratch, and designing customized training scorecards. She conducts skill enhancement workshops and has been successful in developing an understanding and appreciation for the value of measuring and tracking ROI and impact of performance solutions with key executives. Her clients see her work as highly practical and forever changing the way they view their performance solution providers.

Hodges presents her work at conferences and publishes frequently. She is the author of *Linking Learning and Performance* (Butterworth-Heinemann, 2002) and editor of the 1999 *In Action: Measuring Learning and Performance* casebook (ASTD).

Feedback

Although we have made every attempt is made to create the best book possible, we appreciate comments or feedback directly from readers. If you have suggestions or concerns or need additional information, please do not hesitate to contact the authors directly:

Jack Phillips
P.O. Box 380637
Birmingham, AL 35238
205.678.8101
Fax 205.678.8102
Jack@ROIinstitute.net

Patti Phillips
350 Crossbrook Drive
Chelsea, AL 35043
205.678.8101
Fax 205.678.8102
patti@ROIinstitute.net

Toni Hodges
1011 Shore Drive
Edgewater, MD 21037
410.956.0475
Fax 410.956.5436
tonihodges@mindspring.com

Multiblock
Quilt Designs

Pepper Cory

DOVER PUBLICATIONS, INC.
Mineola, New York

Front cover:

Left, *Wanda's Medallion*; center, *The Time Travellers*; right, *Star Wars.*

Photography by Sharon Risedorph, San Francisco, CA

Copyright

Copyright © 1989 by Pepper Cory
All rights reserved under Pan American and International
Copyright Conventions.

Published in Canada by General Publishing Company, Ltd., 30
Lesmill Road, Don Mills, Toronto, Ontario.
Published in the United Kingdom by Constable and Company, Ltd.,
3 The Lanchesters, 162–164 Fulham Palace Road, London W6 9ER.

Bibliographical Note

This Dover edition, first published in 1998, is a slightly altered
republication of *Crosspatch: Inspirations in Multi-Block Quilts,* first published by C&T Publishing, Martinez, CA in 1989. Minor corrections
have been made and the section "Resources" has been omitted.

Library of Congress Cataloging-in-Publication Data

Cory, Pepper.
    Multiblock quilt designs / Pepper Cory.
        p.   cm.
    Originally published: Crosspatch. Martinez, Calif. : C & T Pub.,
1989.
    ISBN 0-486-40047-6 (pbk.)
    1. Patchwork—Patterns. 2. Patchwork quilts. I. Cory, Pepper.
Crosspatch. II. Title.
TT835.C676   1998
746.46'041—dc21   97-50338
                                                            CIP

Manufactured in the United States of America
Dover Publications, Inc., 31 East 2nd Street, Mineola, N.Y. 11501